Buddhist Texts translated from the Pali
With Comments and Introduction
by
Nyanaponika Thera

Buddhist Publication Society
Kandy • Sri Lanka

First edition: 1978
Revised second edition: 1986
Reprint: 2008

The Wheel Publication No. 251/253

Buddhist Publication Society
P.O. Box 61
54 Sangharaja Mawatha
Kandy, Sri Lanka

http://www.bps.lk

National Library of Sri Lanka-Cataloguing in Publication Data

---

Nyanaponika Maha Thera

The Roots of Good and Evil / Nyanaponika Maha Thera.- Kandy: Buddhist Publication Society Inc., 2008. p.120; 18.5 cm

ISBN 978-955-24-0316-3   Price: Rs

i. 294.34435DDC 22   ii. Title
1. Buddhism

Printed by
Creative Printers & Designers,
Bahirawakanda, Kandy.

Contents

Introduction v
I. Basic Explanations 1
II. General Texts 18
III. The Roots and Kamma 28
IV. The Social Significance of the Roots 37
V. The Removal of the Unwholesome Roots 46
VI. Removal through Mindfulness and Insight 73
VII. The Goal 89
VIII. The Roots in the Abhidhamma 92

Introduction

The Buddha has taught that there are three roots of evil: greed, hatred and delusion. These three states comprise the entire range of evil, whether of lesser or greater intensity, from a faint mental tendency to the coarsest manifestations in action and speech. In whatever way they appear, these are the basic causes of suffering.

These roots have their opposites: non-greed, non-hatred and non-delusion. These are the three roots of good: of all acts of unselfishness, liberality and renunciation; of all expressions of loving kindness and compassion; of all achievements in knowledge and understanding.

These six mental states are the roots from which everything harmful and beneficial sprouts. They are the roots of the Tree of Life with its sweet and bitter fruits.

Greed and hatred, maintained and fed by delusion, are the universal impelling forces of all animate life, individually and socially. Fortunately, the roots of good also reach into our world and keep the forces of evil in check, but the balance is a precarious one needing to be preserved by constant watchfulness and effort. On the level of inanimate nature, too, we find counterparts to greed and hatred in the forces of attraction and repulsion, kept in their purposeless reactive movement by inherent nescience which cannot provide a motive for cessation of the process. Thus, through an unfathomable past, the macrocosm of nature and the microcosm of mind have continued their contest between attraction and repulsion, greed and hatred; and unless stopped by voluntary effort and insight, they will so continue for aeons to come. This cosmic conflict of opposing energies, unsolvable on its own level, is one aspect of *dukkha* (unsatisfactoriness): the ill of restless, senseless movement as felt by a sensitive being.

On the human level, too, we see that man, who proudly believes himself to be a "free agent"—the master of his life and even of nature—is in his spiritually undeveloped state actually a passive patient driven about by inner forces he does not recognize. Pulled by his greed and pushed by his hatred, in his blindness he does not see that the brakes for stopping these frantic movements are in his reach, within his own heart. The brakes are the roots of good themselves, which can be cultivated to such a degree that greed, hatred and delusion are utterly destroyed.

Though we have spoken of the six roots as being "roots of good and evil," our use of the terms "good" and "evil" is provisional, a simplification chosen to introduce this teaching by familiar terms. In the Buddhist texts they are called the roots of the wholesome (*kusala-mūla*) and the roots of the unwholesome (*akusala-mūla*). And thus we, too, shall generally call them.

This differentiation of terms marks an important distinction, for the "spread" of the mental states called roots is much wider and deeper than the moral realm to which the words "good" and "evil" refer. The distinction may be defined as follows. An intentional action performed by body or speech is immoral—an evil or a "sin"—when it is motivated by the unwholesome roots and is *intentionally and directly harmful to others*. This constitutes *socially* significant immorality, for which it is the criterion. Such actions are termed *unwholesome bodily* or *verbal kamma*. Thoughts associated with these unwholesome roots, wishing the harm of others, constitute *individually* significant immorality, for which they are the criterion. They include thoughts such as those of injury, murder, theft, fraud and rape, and also false ideologies leading to the harm of others or condoning such harm. Whether or not these thoughts are followed by deeds or words, they constitute *unwholesome mental kamma*.

When greed, hatred and delusion, in any degree, do *not* cause intentional harm to others, they are not evil or immoral in the strict sense of our definition. However, they are still kammically unwholesome in that they maintain bondage and lead to unpleasant results. Similarly, the term "wholesome" extends beyond socially significant morality to comprise also what is individually beneficial, such as acts of renunciation and attempts to understand the nature of reality.

The recent crisis of theistic faith which has taken hold in the West has brought in its trail a moral crisis as well. For many, belief in God has been shattered, and often those who lose their belief in God fail to see any convincing reason for morality without a divine sanction coming down from above. Left without a sound foundation for ethics, they either accept materialistic political ideologies or allow their conduct to be guided by self-interest. Yet we also find today a growing number of people seeking better alternatives. To them the Buddha's teaching on the wholesome and unwholesome roots provides a criterion of good and evil that is neither theological nor authoritarian but experiential, one with a sound psychological basis offering an autonomous pragmatic motivation for avoiding evil and choosing the good.

The social and political motivations for moral conduct proposed to modern man may not openly contradict the basic sentiments of morality, but as their structures are bound to specific historical conditions and reflect the varying self-interests and prejudices of the dominant social group, the values they propose are highly relative, lacking universal validity. In contrast, Buddhist ethics, being based on psychological fact and not on external contingencies, provides a core of moral principles inherently free from relativistic limitations, valid for all time and under all circumstances. By introspection and observation, we can understand that the unwholesome roots are undesirable mental states, productive of suffering for ourselves and others; and since it is our common nature to avoid suffering and to desire happiness, we can understand that it serves our own long-range interest as well as the good of others to restrain actions born of these roots and to act in ways motivated by their wholesome opposites. A brief survey of the evil roots will make this clear.

Greed is a state of lack, need and want. It is always seeking fulfilment and lasting satisfaction, but its drive is inherently insatiable, and thus as long as it endures it maintains the sense of lack.

Hatred, in all its degrees, is also a state of dissatisfaction. Though objectively it arises in response to undesired people or circumstances, its true origins are subjective and internal, chiefly frustrated desire and wounded pride. Buddhist psychology extends the range of hatred beyond simple anger and enmity to include a variety of negative emotions—such as disappointment, dejection, anxiety and despair—representing misguided reactions to the impermanence, insecurity and imperfection inherent in all conditioned existence.

Delusion, taking the form of ignorance, is a state of confusion, bewilderment and helplessness. In its aspect of false views, delusion issues in dogmatism; it takes on a fanatical, even obsessive character, and makes the mind rigid and encapsulated.

All three unwholesome roots lead to inner disharmony and social conflict. In Tibetan paintings they are depicted at the very hub of the Wheel of Life,[1] symbolically represented by a cock, a pig and a snake, turning round and round, catching each other's tails. The three unwholesome roots, indeed, produce and support each other.

The root of greed gives rise to resentment, anger and hatred against those who obstruct the gratification of desire or compete in the chase to gain the desired objects—whether sensual enjoyment, power, dominance or fame. In this way greed leads to conflict

---

1. See *The Wheel of Birth and Death*, Bhikkhu Khantipālo (*Wheel* No.147/149), p.16.

and quarrels. When frustrated, instead of producing enmity and aversion, greed may bring about grief, sadness, despair, envy and jealousy—states which also come under the heading of hatred. The pain of deprivation and frustration again sharpens the keenness of desire, which then seeks an escape from pain by indulging in other kinds of enjoyment.

Both greed and hatred are always linked with delusion. They are grounded upon delusion and, on their part, produce still more delusion as we pursue the objects we desire or flee from those we dislike. Both love and hate blind us to the dangers besetting our pursuits; they lead us away from our true advantage. It is the delusion beneath our love and hate that really blinds us, delusion that leads us astray.

The basic delusion, from which all its other forms spring, is the idea of an abiding self: the belief in an ego. For the sake of this illusory ego men lust and hate; upon this they build their imagination and pride. This ego-belief must first be clearly comprehended as a delusive viewpoint. One must pierce through the illusion of self by cultivating right understanding through penetrative thought and meditative insight.

Though the wholesome and unwholesome roots are individual mental states, their manifestations and repercussions have the greatest social significance. Each individual in society rises up at once to protect himself, his loved ones, his property, security and freedom, from the greed, hatred and delusions of others. His own greed, hatred and ignorance may in turn arouse others to anxious concern and resentment, though he may not be aware of this or care about it. From all this there results an intricate interlocking of suffering—suffering caused to others and suffering experienced oneself. Hence the Buddha repeatedly said that the unwholesome roots cause harm both to oneself and to others, while the wholesome roots are sources of benefit for both the individual and society (see Texts 18–22).

The wholesome and unwholesome roots are of paramount human concern on all levels. As the originating causes of kamma, our life-affirming and rebirth-producing intentional actions, they are the motive powers and driving forces of our deeds, words and thoughts. They mould our character and our destiny and hence determine the nature of our rebirth. Being dominant features in the structure of the mind, the unwholesome roots are used in the Abhidhamma Piṭaka for the classification of unwholesome consciousness and also for a typology of temperaments. All the stages of the path to deliverance are closely concerned with the wholesome and unwholesome roots. At the very beginning, the coarsest forms of greed, hatred and irresponsible ignorance have to be abandoned through virtue (*sīla*), while in the advanced stages the aids of meditation (*samādhi*) and wisdom (*paññā*) have to be applied to a deeper-reaching removal of the unwholesome roots and to the cultivation of the wholesome ones. Even Arahantship and Nibbāna—the consummation of the great quest—are both explained in terms of the roots: as the extinction of greed, hatred and delusion.

This wide-ranging significance of the Buddha's teaching on the roots places it at the very core of the Dhamma. Showing the distinct marks of a fully enlightened mind, it is a teaching simple as well as profound, and hence accessible on many levels. The fact that greed, hatred and delusion, in their extreme forms, are the root causes of much misery and evil should be painfully obvious to every morally sensitive person. Such an initial understanding, open to commonsense, may well grow into full comprehension. It may then become the insight that moves one to enter the path to deliverance—the eradication of greed, hatred and delusion.

Within the framework of the Buddha's teaching, the Roots of Good and Evil have found their place in a great variety of contexts. To illustrate this by an ample selection of Buddhist texts—almost entirely taken from the discourses of the Buddha—is the intention of the following pages.

May progress on that Path prevail and may there be a steady growth of the Roots of Good.

Homage to Him who has seen the Roots of All Things!

> Greed is the root of heedlessness,
> A cause of strife is greed.
> Greed into enslavement drags.
> A hungry ghost one will in future be.
> The Buddha who greed's nature fully knows
> I worship Him, the Greed-free One.

> *Namo te mūla-dassāvī.*
> *Pamādamūlako lobho, lobho vivādamūlako,*
> *dāsabyakārako lobho, lobho paramhi petiko.*
> *Taṃ lobhaṃ parijānantaṃ vande' haṃ vītalobhakaṃ.*

> Hate is the root of turbulence,
> And ugliness results from hate.
> Through hatred much destruction comes,
> To an infernal world one will in future go.
> The Buddha who hate's nature fully knows
> I worship Him, the Hate-free One.

> *Vihaññamūlako doso, doso virūpakārako,*
> *vināsakārako doso, doso paramhi nerayo.*
> *Taṃ dosaṃ parijānantaṃ vande' haṃ vītadosakaṃ.*

> Delusion is the root of all this misery,
> Creator of all ills is ignorant delusion.
> Mind's blindness from delusion stems,
> As a dumb animal one will in future live.
> The Buddha who delusion's nature fully knows
> I worship Him, the Undeluded One.

Sabbāghamūlako moho, moho sabbītikārako,
sabbandhakārako moho, moho paramhi svādiko.
Taṃ mohaṃ parijānantaṃ vande' haṃ vītamohakaṃ.

[A traditional devotional Pali text from Sri Lanka. Source unknown.]

FOR A LONG TIME

Often, O monks, should one reflect upon one's own mind thus: "For a long time has this mind been defiled by greed, by hatred, by delusion." Mental defilements make beings impure, mental cleansing purifies them...

Mind is more multi-featured than a multi-figured painting...

Mind is more variegated than the varieties of animals... Therefore, O monks, should one often reflect upon one's own mind thus: "For a long time has this mind been defiled by greed, by hatred, by delusion." Mental defilements make beings impure, mental cleansing purities them.

SN 22:10

I. Basic Explanations

1. Definitions

There are three roots of the unwholesome: greed, hatred and delusion; and there are three roots of the wholesome: non-greed, non-hatred and non-delusion.

DN 33 (Saṅgīti Sutta)

Comment

These two sets of three are, respectively, the roots of unwholesome and wholesome volitional action (*kamma*), by way of deeds, words or thoughts.

The term "root" (*mūla*), the commentaries explain, has the sense of firm support, cause, condition and producer. The figurative character of the term suggests that the roots can also be taken as conveyors of the "nourishing sap" of the wholesome or unwholesome. They convey this sap to the mental factors and functions existing simultaneously with themselves, as well as to the wholesome or unwholesome actions in which they issue. They are *producers* by being productive of rebirth.

The words "unwholesome" and "wholesome," as used here, are renderings of the Pali terms *akusala* and *kusala*, respectively. Alternative renderings used by other translators are, for the wholesome: profitable, skilful; for the unwholesome: unprofitable, unskilful. The terms "wholesome" and "unwholesome" comprise all volitional actions that bind living beings to saṃsāra, the round of rebirth and suffering. The actions having these roots may, therefore, be called *kammically* wholesome or unwholesome. Hence the range of the unwholesome is wider than that of the immoral, as it includes forms of the root-defilements which are not immoral in the strict sense explained above. The wholesome, as dealt with here and in most, though not all, of the following texts, is that of the mundane type. The wholesome of the supramundane type is not productive of kamma and therefore does not result in rebirth (see Text 17).[1]

The commentators to the Pali scriptures explain *kusala*, the wholesome, as a healthy state of mind (*ārogya*), as morally faultless (*anavajja*), and as having favourable or pleasant kamma-results (*sukha-vipāka*). Another connotation of *kusala*, "dexterous" or "skilful," according to the commentators, does not apply in this context. Yet kammically wholesome actions may also be described as skilful insofar as they lead to happiness in the present and future, and to progress on the path to liberation.

Akusala, the unwholesome, has the opposite characteristics: it is an unhealthy or sickly state of mind (*gelañña*), morally faulty and blameworthy (*sāvajja*), and

---

1. Mundane (*lokiya*) are all those states of consciousness—arising in the worldling as well as in noble ones (*ariya*)—which are not associated with the supramundane paths and fruitions of stream-entry, etc. The supramundane (*lokuttara*) type of the wholesome signifies the four paths and the four fruitions of the stream-enterer, once-returner, non-returner and the Arahat.

has unpleasant kamma-results (*dukkha-vipāka*). For all these reasons, unwholesome actions in thoughts, words and deeds can also be said to be unskilful responses to life.

Of these commentarial explanations, two are derived from a discourse called "The Mantle" (Bāhitika Sutta, Majjhima Nikāya, 88) : namely, "morally faulty" or "faultless" (*sāvajjo, anavajjo*), and 'having unhappy or happy kamma-results" (*dukkha-,sukha-vipāa*). The discourse adds hat the unwholesome brings affliction and harm (*sabyāpajjo*), while the wholesome is free from affliction and harm (*abyāpajjo*). This corresponds to the commentarial description of the unwholesome as an unhealthy state of mind, and of the wholesome as a healthy one.

The Range of the Six Roots

(a) *The Unwholesome.* The three unwholesome roots are not restricted to the strong manifestations suggested by the English terms greed, hatred and delusion. To understand their range it is important to know that in the Pali these three terms stand for all degrees of intensity, even the weakest, of the three defilements, and for all varieties in which these appear. In their weak degrees their unwholesome influence on character and kammic consequences is, of course, not as grave as that of their stronger forms. But even weak forms may carry the risk of either growing stronger or of making a person's character more susceptible to their graver manifestations. A fuller view of the various forms the unwholesome roots assume may be gained from a list of their synonyms, partly taken from the Dhammasaṅgaṇī, the first book of the Abhidhamma Piṭaka.

Greed: liking, wishing, longing, fondness, affection, attachment, lust, cupidity, craving, passion, self-indulgence, possessiveness, avarice; desire for the five sense objects; desire for wealth, offspring, fame, etc.

Hatred: dislike, disgust, revulsion, resentment, grudge, ill-humour, vexation, irritability, antagonism, aversion, anger, wrath, vengefulness.

Delusion: stupidity, dullness, confusion, ignorance of essentials (e.g., the Four Noble Truths), prejudice, ideological dogmatism, fanaticism, wrong views, conceit.

(b) *The Wholesome.* Though formulated negatively, the three wholesome roots signify positive traits:

Non-greed: unselfishness, liberality, generosity; thoughts and actions of sacrifice and sharing; renunciation, dispassion.

Non-hatred: loving kindness, compassion, sympathy, friendliness, forgiveness, forbearance.

Non-delusion: wisdom, insight, knowledge, understanding, intelligence, sagacity, discrimination, impartiality, equanimity.

2. The Commentarial Definitions of the Unwholesome Roots

Greed has the characteristic of grasping an object, like bird-lime (lit. "monkey-lime"). Its function is sticking, like meat put in a hot pan. It is manifested as not giving up, like the dye of lamp-black. Its proximate cause is seeing enjoyment in things that lead to bondage. Swelling with the current of craving, it should be regarded as carrying beings along with it to states of misery as a swift-flowing river does to the great ocean.

Hatred has the characteristic of savageness, like a provoked snake. Its function is to spread, like a drop of poison, or its function is to burn up its own support, like a forest fire. It is manifested as persecuting like an enemy that has got his chance. Its proximate cause is the grounds for annoyance (*āghāta-vatthu*). It should be regarded as being like stale urine mixed with poison.

Delusion has the characteristic of blindness, or it has the characteristic of unknowing. Its function is non-penetration, or its function is to conceal the true nature of an object. It is manifested as the absence of right view,[1] or it is manifested as darkness. Its proximate cause is unwise (unjustified) attention. It should be regarded as the root of all that is unwholesome.

Vism XIV. 162, 171

3. *The Commentarial Definitions of the Wholesome Roots*

Non-greed has the characteristic of the mind's lack of desire for an object, or it has the characteristic of non-adherence, like a water drop on a lotus leaf. Its function

---

1. Comy.: absence of knowledge concerning (the truth of) suffering, etc.

is not to lay hold (or not to grasp), like a liberated bhikkhu. It is manifested as not treating (the desire-evoking object) as a shelter (or non-cleaving), as a man who has fallen into filth (will not cling to it).

Non-hatred has the characteristic of lack of savagery, or the characteristic of non-opposing, like a congenial friend. Its function is to remove annoyance, or its function is to remove fever, as sandalwood does. It is manifested as agreeableness, like the full moon.

Non-delusion has the characteristic of penetrating (things) according to their true nature, or it has the characteristic of sure penetration, like the penetration of an arrow shot by a skilful archer. Its function is to illuminate the objective field, like a lamp. It is manifested as non-bewilderment, like a forest guide. The three should be regarded as the roots of all that is wholesome.

Vism XIV, 143

4. The Nature of the Wholesome Roots

Non-greed is opposed to the taint of avarice; non-hatred to the taint of immorality; non-delusion to an undeveloped state of wholesome qualities.

Non-greed is a condition of giving (*dāna*); non-hatred is a condition of virtue (*sīla*); non-delusion is a condition of mental development (or meditation; *bhāvanā*).

Through *non-greed* one does not overrate (an attractive object), as the lustful person does. Through *non-hatred* one does not underrate or deprecate (an unattractive or disagreeable object), as the hater does. Through non-delusion one has an undistorted view of things, while one who is deluded conceives things in a distorted way.

With *non-greed* one will admit an existing fault (in an attractive object) and will behave accordingly, while a greedy or lustful person will hide that fault. With *non-hatred* one will admit an existing virtue (in a disagreeable or hostile object) and will behave accordingly, while the hater will disparage that virtue. With non-delusion one will admit facts as they are and behave accordingly, while a deluded person holds the true for false (the factual for non-factual) and the false for true (the non-factual for factual).

With *non-greed* one does not have suffering through separation from the beloved; but the greedy and lustful person identifies himself with the beloved and hence cannot bear separation from him. With *non-hatred* one does not have suffering through association with the unbeloved; but the hater identifies himself with (his aversion against) the unbeloved and cannot bear association with him. With *non-delusion* one does not have suffering through not obtaining what one wishes, because the undeluded person will be able to reflect in this way: "How can it be possible that what is subject to decay should not enter into decay?"

With *non-greed* one does not encounter the suffering of birth, because non-greed is the opposite of craving, and craving is at the root of the suffering of birth. With *non-hatred* the suffering of ageing is not felt (strongly, or prematurely); because it is one harbouring strong hate who ages quickly. With *non-delusion* there is no suffering in dying; because it is dying with a confused or deluded mind that is suffering, but this does not happen to one who is undeluded.

Non-greed makes for a happy life among lay people (who often quarrel about property). *Non-delusion* makes for a happy life among ascetics and monks (who often quarrel about opinions). *Non-hatred* makes for happy living with all.

Through *non-greed* there is no rebirth in the realm of the famished ghosts (*peta*); because generally beings are reborn there through their craving, and non-greed (unselfishness, renunciation) is opposed to craving. Through *non-hatred* there is no rebirth in the hells; for it is through hate and a fierce temperament that beings are reborn in hell, which is congenial to hate; but non-hate (loving kindness) is opposed to hate. Through *non-delusion* there is no rebirth in the animal world, for it is generally through delusion that beings are reborn as animals who are always deluded; but non-delusion (wisdom) is opposed to delusion.

Among these three, *non-greed* prevents approach in lust, *non-hatred* prevents alienation through hate, *non-delusion* prevents the loss of equipoise (or impartiality) due to delusion.

Furthermore, to these three roots, in the order given, correspond the following sets of three perceptions: the perception of renunciation, of good will, and of non-violence; and also the perception of bodily foulness, of boundless love and compassion, and of the elements.

Through *non-greed* the extreme of sense-indulgence is avoided; through *non-hatred* the extreme of self-mortification; through *non-delusion* a middle course is practised.

Non-greed breaks the bodily bondage of covetousness, *non-hatred* breaks the bodily bondage of ill-will, and *non-delusion* breaks the other two bondages (i.e., that of clinging to rites and rituals, and of dogmatic fanaticism).

By virtue of the first two wholesome roots, the practice of the first two foundations of mindfulness (i.e., body and feelings) will succeed; by virtue of the third wholesome root (non-delusion), the practice of the last two foundations of mindfulness (state of mind and contents of mind) will succeed.

Non-greed is a condition of health, because one who is not greedy will not partake of something unsuitable, even if it is tempting, and hence he will remain healthy. *Non-hatred* is a condition of youthfulness, because one who is free from hate is not consumed by the fires of hate that cause wrinkles and grey hair, and thus he remains youthful for a long time. *Non-delusion* is a condition of longevity, because one who is undeluded will know what is beneficial and what is harmful, and by avoiding the harmful and resorting to the beneficial he will have a long life.

Non-greed is a condition of the boon of wealth, because one who is not greedy will obtain wealth through his liberality (as its kammic result). *Non-hatred* is a condition of the boon of friendship, because through loving kindness one will win friends and not lose them. *Non-delusion* is a condition of the boon of self-development, because he who is undeluded and does only what is beneficial will perfect himself.

Through *non-greed* one has detachment to persons and things belonging to one's own group; because even in the case of their destruction, one will not feel the suffering that is caused by strong attachment. With *non-hatred*, the same will hold true in the case of persons and things belonging to a hostile group; because one who is free of hatred will have no thoughts of enmity even towards those who are hostile. With *non-delusion*, the same holds true concerning persons and things belonging to a neutral group; because in one who is undeluded there is no strong attachment to anybody or anything.

Through *non-greed* one will understand impermanence; for a greedy person, in his longing for enjoyment, will not see the impermanence of transitory phenomena. Through *non-hatred* one will understand suffering; for one inclined to non-hate, in comprehending the grounds of annoyance discarded by him, sees phenomena as suffering. Through *non-delusion* one will understand not-self; for one who is undeluded is skilled in grasping the nature of reality, and he knows that the five aggregates are without an internal controller. Just as the understanding of impermanence, etc. is effected by non-greed, etc., so are also non-greed, etc. produced by the understanding of impermanence, etc. Through the understanding of impermanence arises non-greed; through the understanding of suffering arises non-hatred; through the understanding of non-self arises non-delusion. For who will allow attachment to arise for something which he fully well knows is impermanent? And, when knowing phenomena to be suffering, who would produce the additional and exceedingly pungent suffering of anger? And, when knowing phenomena as void of self, who would again plunge into confusion of mind?

> From the *Atthasālinī* (commentary to the *Dhammasaṅgaṇī* of the Abhidhamma Piṭaka), pp. 127 ff.

5. The Diversity of the Unwholesome Roots

There may be outsiders, O monks, who will ask you: "There are, friends, three states of mind: greed, hatred and delusion. What is their distinction, their diversity, their difference?"

Questioned thus, O monks, you may explain it to those outsiders in this way:

"Greed is a lesser fault and fades away slowly; hatred is a great fault and fades away quickly; delusion is a great fault and fades away slowly."

> AN 3:68 (extract)

Comment

The statements in this text about greed being a lesser fault, and so on, have to be taken in a relative sense. The commentary explains: "Greed (or lust) is a lesser fault in a twofold way: (1) in public opinion (*loka*; i.e., in the 'eyes of the world'), and (2) with regard to kamma-result (*vipāka*), i.e., the rebirth resulting from the kamma (impelled by greed).

"(1) If, for instance, parents give their children in marriage, according to the standards of worldly life no fault is involved (though greed enters into the parents' affection and sexuality in marriage).

"(2) If in marriage one is satisfied with one's own marriage-partner (and thus observes the third percept), there is thereby no rebirth in the lower worlds. Thus greed or lust can be a lesser fault in regard to kamma-result. Greed, however, is 'slow in fading away,' being as hard to remove as oily soot. Greed for particular objects or sensual lust for a certain person may persist throughout life. It may even continue for two or three existences without disappearing."

Thus, relative to hatred and delusion, greed is a lesser evil. For if it remains within the bounds of basic morality, and does not entail a violation of the five precepts, it will not exclude a favourable rebirth caused by good kamma. Greed, however, is very hard to overcome entirely. Its fine hair-roots reach deep into our nature, and it may clad itself in many alluring garments, assuming subtle disguises and sublime forms of beauty. As "lust for life" or "the will to live" it is the very core of existence. As life-affirming craving it is the origin of suffering.

"Hatred," according to the commentary, "may lead to wrong-doings towards parents, brothers, sisters, ascetics (i.e., people of religious calling), etc. Wherever such an offender goes, blame and bad reputation will follow him. If, through hatred, he even commits one of the heinous offences (*ānantariya-kamma*), such as parricide, etc., he will suffer in hell for aeons.[1] In that way, hatred is a great fault both in public opinion and by its kamma-result. Yet hatred may quickly fade away; for soon after committing an offence out of hatred or anger one may repent, ask those whom one has wronged for forgiveness, and if that is granted, the act is atoned for (as far as the offender's state of mind is concerned.)"

Hatred is a disruptive and anti-social factor, a source of untold misery for individuals and all human groups. One would thus expect society to regard it as a "great fault," as the great enemy of societal welfare, and make every effort to weaken and eliminate it. But on the contrary we find that human institutions, large and small, have often promoted hate for their own selfish ends, or have fostered deeds, words and thoughts of hate motivated by delusive ideologies. Throughout history, leaders seeking the support of the masses have always found it easier to unite people by means of a common hate than by a common love.

On the individual level, hatred in all its degrees is often roused by conflicting self-interests and by other kinds of egocentric antagonism. Hatred can grow as obsessive as lustful passion, but it is generally more

---

1. The Buddhist scriptures speak of five "heinous offences"—parricide, matricide, killing an Arahat, wounding a Buddha and maliciously causing a schism in the Sangha.

destructive for both the hater and his victim. It can take deep roots in the mind, be it in the form of smouldering resentment or the enjoyment of outbursts of violence. Through hatred, man's mind may sink to a sub-human level, and thus for the hater there is always the risk of being reborn in a sub-human realm of existence.

Yet for one who does not identify himself with all his states of mind, but sees the need and has the will to transform himself—for such a one it will not be difficult to control his hatred or anger before it grows stronger. Hatred causes irritation, tension and distress; and since human beings are basically "desirous of happiness and averse to unhappiness," those who do understand the consequences of hatred will normally wish to get rid of it.

"Delusion," according to the commentary, "is a great fault for both reasons, that is, in the eyes of public opinion and with regard to its unhappy kamma-result (in the same ways as mentioned above for hatred). If an action is done under the impact of delusion, such action will set one free only very slowly; it can be likened to a bear skin, which will not become bright even if washed seven times."

If unrestrained acts of unlawful greed or lust are performed without a feeling of guilt, but are, on the contrary, justified by such prejudiced views as the claim that might makes right, such deluded greed will obviously not be easy to eliminate. It will not be given up even under the impact of repeated failures to satisfy it, which may only strengthen the greed through frustration and resentment. There are also forms of deluded greed supported by a religious (or pseudo-religious) sanction (see Comment to Text 17). All these forms of deluded greed can be eliminated only when the delusive false views and principles are discarded. But even in cases where greed is not backed by wrong theory, when self-indulgence has the uninhibited innocence of ignorance or when the delusive view involved is just the naive belief that "this is the right and natural thing to do"—in these cases, too, our bondage by such deluded greed will be hard to break.

It is similar when delusion instigates hatred and keeps it alive with wrong views or attitudes. If, for instance, due to delusive views, people regard others belonging to certain races, classes or religions as legitimate objects of hate, this will be a much stronger bondage than any impassioned but temporary outburst of anger having only the normal admixture of delusion.

Without the presence of delusion, no greed or hatred can arise. The unwholesome roots of greed and hatred always occur associated with delusion. Delusion, however, may occur by itself and can be a very powerful source of evil and suffering. In view of that omnipresence of delusion in the unwholesome, the Dhammapada says that there is no entanglement equal to the widespread net of delusion (v. 251), and that ignorance (a synonym of delusion) is the greatest taint of the mind (v. 243). Hence the Buddha declares: "All unwholesome states have their root in ignorance, they converge upon ignorance, and by the abolishing of ignorance, all the other unwholesome states are abolished." (SN 20:1)

Ignorance, of course, does not mean a mere lack of information about this or that subject of worldly knowledge. It is, rather, the lack of right understanding concerning the Four Noble Truths: namely, the ignorance (or wilful ignoring) of the full range and depth of suffering, of its true cause, of the fact that there can be an end of suffering and of the path that leads to the end of suffering.

The truth of suffering is hidden by the four distortions of reality (*vipallāsa*), the four great illusions of seeing permanence in the impermanent, happiness in what is truly suffering, selfhood in what is void of a self, and beauty in the unbeautiful. These distortions, powerful universal manifestations of ignorance and delusion, shut out an understanding of the truth of suffering, and thereby obscure the other truths, too. The four may appear on any of three levels: at the level of quite ordinary misperceptions (*saññā-vipallāsa*), or as wrong ways of thinking (*citta-vipallāsa*), or as expressed in definite wrong ideas and theories (*diṭṭhi-vipallāsa*). Tenaciously held wrong views can forge the strongest chain fettering beings to pain-fraught saṃsāra. If these views go so far as to deny the moral relevance of any action, they will lead in the next existence to a "fixed destiny" of rebirth in a world of misery.[1]

Sheer stupidity is, of course, also a form of

---

1. On "wrong views with fixed result" (*niyata-micchā-diṭṭhi*), see Apaṇṇaka Sutta (*Wheel* No. 98/99), p. 23.

delusion, and it can stultify a person's inner growth throughout life and for many lives to come. But there can be an escape from it, if that dull person's good roots of non-greed (selflessness) and non-hate (kindness, compassion) are strong enough to become active.

The most deep-rooted and powerful aspect of delusion, and the most consequential of wrong views, is personality-belief. Personality-belief is the belief in an abiding self or soul, with its attendant conceits and conceptions. The belief may be naive and unreflective, or supported by definite theories and convictions. But however it is held, this personality-belief makes delusion a barrier hard to overcome and slow to fade away, while the moral implications of egocentricity make it a "great fault."

Considering the wide range and universal influence of delusion, it is understandable that, under the name of ignorance, it appears as the first factor in the chain of dependent origination (*paṭicca-samuppāda*). As the chief impelling force that keeps the wheel of existence in rotation, delusion is indeed "a great fault and slow to fade away."

II. General Texts

6. *Overcoming Birth and Death*

If three things were not found in the world, the Perfect One, the Holy One who is fully enlightened, would not appear in the world, nor would his teaching and discipline shed their light over the world.

What are these three things? They are birth, old age and death. Because these three are found in the world, the Perfect One, the Holy One who is fully enlightened, has appeared in the world, and his teaching and discipline shed their light over the world.

It is, however, impossible to overcome birth, old age and death without overcoming another three things, namely: greed, hatred and delusion.

AN 10:76

7. *Bondage and Freedom*

There are two things:[1] seeing enjoyment in things that can fetter,[2] and seeing dissatisfaction[3] in things that can fetter.

---

1. Or two kinds of outlook.
2. *Saṃyojaniyesu dhammesu assādānupassitā.* Comy: things which are conditions for the ten fetters (*saṃyojana*).
3. Or revulsion, disgust; *saṃyojaniyesu dhammesu nibbidānupassitā.*

He who lives seeing enjoyment in things that can fetter cannot give up greed, hatred and delusion; and without giving them up be will not be freed from birth, old age and death, not from sorrow, lamentation, pain, grief and despair; he will not be freed from suffering, this I declare. But he who lives seeing dissatisfaction in things that can fetter will give up greed, hatred and delusion; and by giving them up he will be freed from birth, old age and death, from sorrow, lamentation, pain, grief and despair; he will be freed from suffering, this I declare.

Aṅguttara Nikāya, 2: 6

8. Barbs

Greed is a barb, hatred is a barb, and delusion is a barb. Hence, monks, you should abide without (these) barbs, abide free from (these) barbs. Without (such) barbs are the Arahats, free from (such) barbs are the Arahats.

Aṅguttara Nikāya, 10; 72

Comment

The Pāli word for "barb" is *kaṇṭaka*, literally "a thorn." A similar figurative expression, that of a dart (*salla*), occurs in the Suttanipāta:

> *I saw what is so hard to see,*
> *the dart embedded in the heart—*
> *the dart by which afflicted we*

hurry on in all directions.
If once this dart has been removed,
one will not hurry, will not sink.

(vv. 938–939)

9. From the Mahā-Vedalla Sutta

Greed is a producer of limitations, hatred is a producer of limitations, delusion is a producer of limitations.*

Greed is something burdensome, hatred is something burdensome, delusion is something burdensome.**

Greed is a maker of (tainted) marks. hatred is a maker of (tainted) marks, delusion is a maker of (tainted) marks.*** All these are given up by the taint-free Arahat; they are out off at the root, made barren like a palm-stump, brought to non-existence, no longer liable to arise again in the future.

Majjhima Nikāya 43

Comments

* "Producer of limitations" (*pamāṇa-karaṇa*). The three roots of evil limit man's outlook, place limitations on his vision of things as they really are, and limit his potential freedom of choice. As the subcommentary says, they make for a "shallow and narrow mentality" (*uttāno paritta-cetaso*).

The commentary explains differently, saying that the manifestations of the three unwholesome roots provide a standard or criterion (*pamāṇa*) for judging whether people are unliberated worldlings (*puthujjana*) or noble persons (*ariya*). But as this text later contrasts this term with *appamāṇa-cetovimutti*, the "boundless liberation of the mind," the interpretation chosen here appears more probable.

** "Something burdensome" (*kiñcana*). The Pāli word *kiñcana* means "something," In another passage of the same text (not reproduced here), this is contrasted with *ākiñcañña-cetovimutti*, the "liberation of mind through (the meditative state of) nothingness." The commentary, however, relates the word to a verb *kiñchati*, "to crush, press down, oppress." Greed, hatred and delusion are certainly a heavy burden, pressing man down by "something or other" that evokes his passions and clouds his vision. The term *kiñcana* sometimes also has the meaning of property or possessions.

*** "Maker of (tainted) marks," (*nimitta-karaṇa*). The three unwholesome roots impress, as it were, their marks upon the objects of sense perception; hence these objects are habitually identified as attractive and repulsive, or as bases evoking confusion and wrong views. The roots also attach to "self and world" the delusive marks of permanence, happiness, selfhood and beauty instead of the true marks of impermanence, liability to suffering, not-self and impurity.

10. Māra's Prisoner [1]

He who has not abandoned greed, hatred and delusion, is called Māra's prisoner, captured in Māra's snares, subject to the Evil One's will and pleasure.

But he who has abandoned greed, hatred and delusion, is no longer Māra's prisoner; he is freed from Māra's snares, no longer subject to the Evil One's will and pleasure.

It 68

11. Crossing the Ocean

A monk or a nun who has not abandoned greed, hatred and delusion, such a one has not crossed the ocean (of saṃsāra), with its waves and whirlpools, monsters and demons.

But a monk or a nun who has abandoned greed, hatred and delusion, such a one has crossed the ocean (of saṃsāra), with its waves and whirlpools, monsters and demons, has traversed it and gone to the other shore (Nibbāna), standing on firm ground as a true saint.

It 69

12. The Three Fires

There are three fires: the fire of lust, the fire of hatred and the fire of delusion.

---

1. Māra: the personification of the forces antagonistic to enlightenment.

The fire of lust burns lustful mortals
Who are entangled in the sense-objects.
The fire of hate burns wrathful men
Who urged by hate slay living beings.
Delusion's fire burns foolish folk
Who cannot see the holy Dhamma.

Those who delight in the embodied group[1]
Do not know this triple fire.
They cause the worlds of woe to grow:
The hells, and life as animal,
The ghostly and demoniac realms;
Unfreed are they from Māra's chains.

But those who live by day and night
Devoted to the Buddha's law,
They quench within the fire of lust
By seeing the impurity of body.

They quench within the fire of hate
By loving kindness, loftiest of men.
Delusion's fire they also quench
By wisdom ripening in penetration.[2]
When they extinguish these three fires,

---

1. The term "embodied group" (*sakkāya*) refers to the transient personality consisting of the five aggregates: body, feeling, perception, mental formations and consciousness.

2. Literally, "leading to the piercing" (*nibbedha-gāminī*). This refers to the piercing, or destroying, of the mass of defilements.

Wise, unremitting day and night,
Completely they are liberated,
Completely they transcend all ill.

Seers of the holy realm,[1]
Through perfect knowledge[2] wise,
By direct vision ending all rebirth,
They do not go to any new existence.

It 93

From the Commentary by Bhadantācariya Dhammapāla

Because greed, when it arises, burns and consumes living beings, it is called a fire; and so it is with hatred and delusion. Just as a fire consumes the fuel through which it has arisen, and grows into a vast conflagration, similarly it is with greed, hatred and delusion: they consume the life-continuity in which they have arisen and grow into a vast conflagration that is hard to extinguish.

Innumerable are the beings who, with hearts ablaze with the fire of lust, have come to death through the suffering of unfulfilled desire. This is greed's burning power. For the burning power of hatred, a special example is the "deities ruined by their angry minds" (*manopadosika-devā*), and for delusion, the "deities

---
1. The "holy realm" is Nibbāna.
2. "Through perfect knowledge" (*sammad-aññāya*). *Aññā* is the highest knowledge, or gnosis, attained by Arahatship.

ruined by their playful pleasures" (*khiḍḍapadosika-devā*).[1] In their delusion, the latter become so forgetful that they miss their meal-time and die. This is the burning power of greed, hatred and delusion, as far as the present life is concerned. In future lives these three are still more terrible and hard to endure, in so far as greed, etc., may cause rebirth in the hells and the other worlds of woe.

13. Three Inner Foes

There are three inner taints, three inner foes, three inner enemies, three inner murderers, three inner antagonists. What are these three? Greed is an inner taint.... Hatred is an inner taint.... Delusion is an inner taint, an inner foe, an inner enemy, an inner murderer, an inner antagonist.

> *Greed is a cause of harm,*
> *Unrest of mind it brings.*
> *This danger that has grown within,*
> *Blind folk are unaware of it.*
>
> *A greedy person cannot see the facts,*
> *Nor can he understand the Dhamma.*
> *When greed has overpowered him,*
> *In complete darkness he is plunged.*

---

1. The former die and fall away from their heaven because of anger, the latter because of their negligence. See the Brahmajāla Sutta (DN 1).

*But he who does not crave and can forsake
This greed and what incites to greed,
From him quickly greed glides off
Like water from a lotus leaf.*

*Hate is a cause of harm,
Unrest of mind it brings.
This danger that has grown within,
Blind folk are unaware of it.*

*A hater cannot see the facts,
Nor can he understand the Dhamma.
When hate has overpowered him,
In complete darkness he is plunged.*

*But he who does not hate and can forsake
This hatred and what incites to hate,
From him quickly hatred falls off
As from a palm tree falls the ripened fruit.*

*Delusion is a cause of harm,
Unrest of mind it brings.
This danger that has grown within,
Blind folk are unaware of it.*

*He who is deluded cannot see the facts,
Nor can he understand the Dhamma.
If a man is in delusion's grip,
In complete darkness he is plunged.*

*But he who has shed delusion's veil
Is undeluded where confusion reigns;
He fully scatters all delusion,
Just as the sun dispels the night.*

It 88

Comment

Greed, hatred and delusion strong enough to lead to sub-human rebirth are abandoned by the first path, that of stream-entry. Sensual desire and hatred, in their coarse forms, are abandoned by the second path (of once-return), and in their subtle forms, by the third path (of non-return). All remaining greed and delusion, along with their associated defilements, are abandoned by the fourth path—that of Arahatship.

III. The Roots and Kamma

14. The Causes of Action

There are, O monks, three causes for the origin of action (*kamma*): greed, hatred and delusion.

From greed, O monks, no greedlessness will arise; it is greed that arises from greed. From hatred no hatelessness will arise; it is hatred that arises from hatred. From delusion no non-delusion will arise; it is delusion that arises from delusion.

Due to actions born of greed, born of hatred, born of delusion, neither divine beings will appear, nor humans, nor any other kind of happy existence.[1] Rather the hells, the animal kingdom, the realm of ghosts or some other kind of woeful existence will appear due to actions born of greed, hatred and delusion.

These are, O monks, three causes for the origin of action.

There are, O monks, three other causes for the origin of action: non-greed, non-hatred and non-delusion.

From non-greed, O monks, no greed will arise; it is non-greed that arises from non-greed. From non-hatred no hatred will arise; it is non-hatred that arises from non-hatred. From non-delusion no delusion will arise; it is non-delusion that arises from non-delusion.

Due to actions born of non-greed, non-hatred and non-delusion, neither the hells will appear, nor the animal kingdom, nor the realm of ghosts, nor any other

---

1. By way of rebirth.

kind of woeful existence. Rather divine beings, humans or some other kind of happy existence will appear due to actions born of non-greed, non-hatred and non-delusion.

These are, O monks, three other causes for the origin of action.

AN 6:39

Comment

In this text the Buddha implicitly rejects the maxim that "the end justifies the means"—a doctrine widely followed in politics and sometimes even by religious institutions. Our text further declares as groundless the hope of those who apply this maxim in the belief that they will be rewarded in a future life for serving their cause by unrighteous means in this life, or in the case of non-religious application, that a future generation will reap the reward of present violence and repression in an ideal society or "paradise on earth."

Our text further negates the notion that lustful passion, or actions usually regarded as immoral or sinful, need not be obstacles to liberation or salvation, and can even aid their attainment. Such ideas, in varying formulations, have been mooted in the antinomian sects belonging to several of the world's great religions.[1] The notion that the end justifies the

---

1. For a fuller repudiation of this thesis in the Buddha's own time, see *The Snake Simile* (MN 22), tr. by Nyanaponika Thera (Wheel No. 48/49), pp. 13, 16, 39.

means occurs also in the basic principle of the intentional theory of ethics: "Whatever is done with the intention of doing good to the world is right or virtuous." All such notions, the Buddha's statement implies, are untenable, undermined by the deep psychological connections of the roots.

15. The Ten Ways of Action

If a noble disciple knows what is unwholesome and knows the root of the unwholesome; if he knows what is wholesome and knows the root of the wholesome—he is then, to that extent, one of right understanding; he is one whose understanding is correct, who has firm confidence in the teaching, and has arrived at (the core of) the good Dhamma.

And what is unwholesome? Killing is unwholesome, taking what is not given is unwholesome, sexual misconduct is unwholesome; lying is unwholesome, tale-bearing is unwholesome, harsh language is unwholesome, vain talk is unwholesome; covetousness is unwholesome, ill-will is unwholesome, wrong views are unwholesome.

And what is the root of the unwholesome? Greed is a root of the unwholesome, hatred is a root of the unwholesome, delusion is a root of the unwholesome.

And what is wholesome? Abstaining from killing is wholesome, abstaining from taking what is not given is wholesome, abstaining from sexual misconduct is wholesome; abstaining from lying ... from tale-bearing ... from harsh language ... from vain talk is wholesome;

non-covetousness is wholesome, non-ill-will is wholesome, right understanding is wholesome.

And what is the root of the wholesome? Non-greed is a root of the wholesome, non-hatred is a root of the wholesome, non-delusion is a root of the wholesome.

MN 9 (Sammādiṭṭhi Sutta)

Comment

In this discourse, spoken by the venerable Sāriputta, the unwholesome and the wholesome are explained by the "ten ways of unwholesome and wholesome action" (*akusala-kusala-kammapatha*), which extend to deeds, words and thoughts. They are also called the ten bad and ten good ways of conduct.

This explanation of the unwholesome enumerates ten cases of definite immoral behaviour. Even the last three items, referring to unwholesome *mental* kamma, have in this context an immoral character. As ways of unwholesome mental action, they signify the covetous desire to appropriate others' property; the hateful thoughts of harming, hurting or killing others; and those wrong views which deny moral causality and thus give room and justification for immoral acts.

These ten, however, do not exhaust the range of the term *unwholesome*. As mentioned earlier, the range of the unwholesome is wider than that of the immoral. It is not restricted to violations of the ten bad courses, but comprises all deeds, words and thoughts motivated by any degree of greed, hate and delusion.

To give a few examples: fondness for good food, music or physical comfort is not immoral, but as an attachment which binds us to the world of sense experience, it is kammically unwholesome. The same holds true for sexual acts, words and thoughts directed to one's marriage partner. These, too, according to the moral code of lay society, are not immoral. Yet as strong manifestations of craving, they fall under the unwholesome root "greed." One's personal stupidity, narrowness of view, ignorance of what is truly beneficial and similar limitations of mind are not immoral and need not have immediate immoral consequences. Yet they are great impediments to the acquisition of liberating wisdom and bind one firmly to saṃsāra. Therefore, they too are unwholesome, being forms of the unwholesome root "delusion."

16. The Roots of the Ten Unwholesome Ways

Killing, I declare, O monks, is of three kinds: motivated by greed, motivated by hatred, motivated by delusion.

Also the taking of what is not given, sexual misconduct, lying, tale-bearing, harsh language, vain talk, covetousness, ill-will and wrong views—all these, I declare, are of three kinds: motivated by greed, motivated by hatred, motivated by delusion.

Thus, O monks, greed is an originator of the kamma-concatenation, hatred is an originator of the kamma-concatenation, delusion is an originator of the kamma-concatenation. But by the destruction of greed, hatred and delusion, the kamma-concatenation comes to an end.

AN 10:174

17. Rebirth and its Cessation

I

There are, O monks, three causes for the origin of action: greed, hatred and delusion.

An action performed out of greed, born of greed, caused by greed, originating in greed;

an action performed out of hatred, born of hatred, caused by hatred, originating in hatred;

an action performed out of delusion, born of delusion, caused by delusion, originating in delusion—

such an action will ripen wherever the individual is reborn; and wherever the action ripens, there the individual will reap the fruit thereof, be it in this life, in the next or in future lives.

It is as with seeds that are undamaged and unspoiled, unimpaired by wind and heat, capable of sprouting, sown well in a good field, planted in well-prepared soil. If there is plentiful rain, these seeds will come to growth, increase and reach full development. Similarly, an action performed out of greed, hatred or delusion will ripen wherever the individual is reborn; and wherever the action ripens, the individual will reap the fruit thereof, be it in this life, in the next life or in future lives.

II

There are three other causes for the origin of action: non-greed, non-hatred and non-delusion.

If an action is performed out of non-greed, born of non-greed, caused by non-greed, originating in non-greed, and if greed has entirely gone;

if performed out of non-hatred, born of non-hatred, caused by non-hatred, originating in non-hatred, and if hatred has entirely gone;

if performed out of non-delusion, born of non-delusion, caused by non-delusion, originating in non-delusion, and if delusion has entirely gone—

such an action is thereby given up, cut off at its root, made (barren) like a palm-stump, brought to non-existence and is no longer liable to arise in the future again.

It is as with seeds that are undamaged and unspoiled, unimpaired by wind and heat, capable of sprouting, sown well in a good field. If now a man were to burn them, reduce them to ashes and then scatter the ashes in a strong wind or throw them into a stream's rapid current which carried them away—then these seeds would have been utterly destroyed, made unable to sprout again.

Similarly, if an action is performed out of non-greed, non-hatred and non-delusion, and if greed, hatred and delusion have entirely gone—such an action is thereby given up, cut off at its root, made (barren) like a palm-stump, brought to non-existence and is no longer liable to arise in the future again.

AN 3:33

Comment on Section II

Greed and delusion in their weaker forms are entirely eliminated on attaining Arahatship, while hatred down to its weakest form is fully abandoned at the stage of the non-returner. Section II of our text applies, therefore, only to actions performed at these stages of final emancipation. Only then are these actions finally "given up" so that they can no longer lead to a future rebirth. It is thus only at Arahatship that all three unwholesome roots are "entirely gone," though they are decisively weakened at the earlier three stages of emancipation.

The Arahat's action, as no longer productive of rebirth, occurs also as the fourth item in a fourfold division of kamma:

Dark action that brings dark results;

bright action that brings bright results;

partly bright and partly dark action which brings partly bright and partly dark results;

action neither bright nor dark which brings neither bright nor dark results and leads to the exhaustion of action.

AN 4:232; MN 57

The text explains that this last type of action is the volition of giving up all acts of kammic formation, that is, the volition present in the states of consciousness pertaining to the four paths of emancipation. But this fourth type can also be understood as the actions an Arahat performs in ordinary life, for these do not lead him into kammic involvement or bind him to a future rebirth. His good actions may appear quite similar to the moral deeds of noble (though unliberated) worldlings, but the Arahat's actions are not motivated by the slightest trace of craving and ignorance. In the Arahat's mind there is no greed (craving) by way of wishing that his virtue be recognized and appreciated, no delusion (ignorance) by way of a proud satisfaction in "being good," no illusionary expectations as to the result of these good actions; nor is there any other self-reference in any form whatever. An Arahat's good actions are a spontaneous outflow of a fully purified mind and heart, responding without hesitation to situations where help is needed and possible. But though his actions may be inspired by sympathy and compassion, beneath them there is detachment and deep serenity instead of emotional involvement. As long as the momentum of his life-force lasts, the Arahat lives on as an embodiment of wisdom and compassion. But as the Arahat's mind no longer clings to anything, not even to the results of his actions, there is no potentiality left for any future rebirth. The life-nourishing sap conveyed by the roots has ceased to flow, and the roots of continued existence themselves are cut off.

IV. The Social Significance of the Roots

18. *From the Kālāma Sutta*

"What do you think, Kālāmas? When greed, hatred and delusion arise in a person, is it for his benefit or harm?"—"For his harm, venerable sir."—"Kālāmas, a person who is greedy, hating and deluded, overpowered by greed, hatred and delusion, his thoughts controlled by them, will take life, take what is not given, indulge in sexual misconduct, and tell lies; he will also prompt others to do likewise. Will that conduce to his harm and his suffering for a long time?"—"Yes, venerable sir."

"What do you think, Kālāmas? Are these things wholesome or unwholesome?"—"Unwholesome, venerable sir."—"Blamable or blameless?"—"Blamable, venerable sir."—"Censured or praised by the wise?"—"Censured, venerable sir."—"Undertaken and practised, do these things lead to harm and suffering, or not? Or how is it in this case?"—"Undertaken and practised, these things lead to harm and suffering. So does it appear to us in this case."

"Therefore, Kālāmas, did we say: Do not go upon repeated hearing (of orally transmitted religious tradition), nor upon a linear succession (of teachers), nor upon hearsay, nor upon the authority of scriptures, nor upon speculative and logical grounds, nor upon thought-out theories, nor on preference for views pondered upon, nor upon another's seeming competence, nor on the consideration that 'The monk is our teacher.'

"But when you yourselves know: 'These things are unwholesome, blamable, censured by the wise, and if undertaken and practised they will lead to harm and suffering,' then give them up."

AN 3:65

19. Why Give Up the Roots of Evil?

Once a wandering ascetic, Channa by name, visited the venerable Ānanda and spoke to him as follows:

"You, friend Ānanda, teach the giving up of greed, hatred and delusion, and we, too, teach it. But, friend Ānanda, what disadvantage have you seen in greed, hatred and delusion that you teach that they ought to be given up?"

"Friend, a person who is greedy, hating and deluded, overpowered by greed, hatred and delusion, his thoughts controlled by them, aims at his own harm, aims at others' harm, aims at the harm of both, and he suffers pain and grief in his mind. But when greed, hatred and delusion are given up, he will not aim at his own harm, nor at the harm of others, nor at the harm of both, and he will not suffer pain and grief in his mind.

"A person who is greedy, hating and deluded, overpowered by greed, hatred and delusion, his thoughts controlled by them, leads an evil way of life in deeds, words and thoughts; he does not know his own true advantage, nor that of others, nor that of both. But when greed, hatred and delusion are given up, he will not lead an evil way of life in deeds, words and thoughts; and he will understand his own true advantage, that of others, and that of both.

"Greed, hatred and delusion, friend, make one blind, unseeing and ignorant; they destroy wisdom, are bound up with distress, and do not lead to Nibbāna.

"Because we have seen these disadvantages in greed, hatred and delusion, therefore, friend, do we teach that they ought to be given up.

"This Noble Eightfold Path, namely: right understanding, right thought, right speech, right action, right livelihood, right effort, right mindfulness and right concentration—this, friend, is the path, the way to the giving up of greed, hatred and delusion."

AN 3:71

20. *The Visible Teaching*

"People speak of the 'visible teaching.' In how far, Lord, is the teaching visible here and now, of immediate result, inviting to come and see, onward-leading, to be directly experienced by the wise?"

"A person who is greedy, hating and deluded, overpowered by greed, hatred and delusion, aims at his own harm, at others' harm, at the harm of both, and he suffers pain and grief in his mind. He also leads an evil way of life in deeds, words and thoughts, and he does not know his own true advantage, that of others and that of both.

"But when greed, hatred and delusion are given up, he will not aim at his own harm, at others' harm, at the harm of both, and he will not suffer pain and grief in his mind. He will not lead an evil life and he will understand his own true advantage, that of others and that of both.

"In that sense is the teaching visible here and now, of immediate result, inviting to come and see, onward-leading, to be directly experienced by the wise."

AN 3:53

Comment

The description of the teaching (Dhamma) as being "visible here and now" and so forth, is the same as in the traditional text of homage to the Dhamma.

The Dhamma taught by the Buddha is the Four Noble Truths. If that Dhamma is here identified with the teaching on the unwholesome roots and their abandonment, we may understand the connection thus: the presence of greed, hate and delusion corresponds to the truths of suffering and its origin, their abandonment to the truths of the path and its goal, Nibbāna, the cessation of suffering.

When, through earnest effort in practising the Dhamma, one succeeds in weakening the evil roots, the truth of the teaching becomes clearly visible. The Dhamma indeed yields immediate results. Having accepted its invitation to "come and see," one has tested it and seen its benefits for oneself. Encouraged by these partial results, one will be led onwards towards the goal—the final eradication of greed, hatred and delusion. But the experience has to be personal—gone through by each one himself, alone, through wisdom and energy devoted to the work of liberation.

21. Four Types of People

There are four types of people in the world. One who works for his own good, but not for the good of others; one who works for the good of others, but not for his own good; one who works neither for his own good nor for the good of others; and one who works for his own good as well as for the good of others.

And which is the person who works for his own good, but not for the good of others? It is he who strives for the abolishing of greed, hatred and delusion in himself, but does not encourage others to abolish greed, hatred and delusion.

And which is the person who works for the good of others, but not for his own good? It is he who encourages others to abolish greed, hatred and delusion, but does not strive for the abolishing of greed, hatred and delusion in himself.

And which is the person who works neither for his own good nor for the good of others? It is he who neither strives for the abolishing of greed, hatred and delusion in himself, nor encourages others to abolish greed, hatred and delusion.

And which is the person who works for his own good as well as for the good of others? It is he who strives for the abolishing of greed, hatred and delusion in himself, and also encourages others to abolish greed, hatred and delusion.

AN 4:76

22. The Roots of Violence and Oppression

There are, O monks, three roots of the unwholesome: greed, hatred and delusion.

Greed, hatred and delusion of every kind are unwholesome. Whatever kamma a greedy, hating and deluded person heaps up, by deeds, words or thoughts, that, too, is unwholesome.[1] Whatever suffering such a person, overpowered by greed, hatred and delusion, his thoughts controlled by them, inflicts under false pretexts[2] upon another—by killing, imprisonment, confiscation of property, false accusations or expulsion, being prompted in this by the thought, "I have power and I want power"—all this is unwholesome too. In this manner, there arise in him many evil unwholesome states of mind, born of and originating from greed, hatred and delusion, caused and conditioned by greed, hatred and delusion.

AN 3:69

---

1. The verb *abhisaṅkharoti*, "heaps up," refers to kammic accumulation through the volitional kamma-formations (*saṅkhāra*), which are here of an unwholesome character. The commentary emphasizes the fact that greed, hate and delusion are not only unwholesome in themselves, but also roots of future unwholesome evil conditions.
2. *Asatā*; lit.: falsely, untruthfully.

Comment

As our text vividly shows, the three roots of evil have dreadful repercussions on society, as causes of cruelty and the infliction of suffering. The Buddha speaks of the three as motives for the unrestrained use of power, and the examples given in the text make it clear that he refers to political power: a ruler's abuse of power whether in time of war against his country's enemy, or in peacetime towards its own population. During his lifetime, the Buddha must have observed many cases of violence and oppression. He also must have known that the false pretexts justifying such abuses of power are used in war as well as in peace. False propaganda against a country's enemy, and slander of the chosen victims in the ruler's own country, obviously existed even 2500 years ago. In fact, all those instances of violence and oppression mentioned by the Buddha have quite a familiar ring today. And, of course, the driving forces behind them are still the same: greed, hatred and delusion. In modern history, however, the central role has shifted towards delusion, which runs beneath various aggressive ideologies of a religious, political or racial character.

The Buddha may have been recalling his life as a prince at his father's court when he spoke those moving verses opening the sutta called "The Use of Violence" (Attadaṇḍa Sutta):

The use of violence breeds terror:
See the nation embroiled in strife!
How this has moved my heart,
How I was stirred, I shall now tell.

Seeing the crowds in frantic movement,
Like swarms of fish when the pond dries up;
Seeing how people fight each other,
By fear and horror I was struck.

Sn vv. 935–36

Only rarely did the Buddha speak about those darker sides of contemporary society, but these few texts show that he was a keen and compassionate observer.

Generally, all three roots of evil operate in those acts of violence and oppression which our text mentions. But in specific cases any of the three might be dominant, though an element of delusion, or ignorance, will always be present. In war, rulers might be motivated chiefly by greed for territory, wealth, economic dominance or political supremacy; but to make the war popular among their own people, they will employ hate-propaganda to whip up their will to fight. Delusion was a prominent motive in the religious wars of the past, and in our present time it still crops up in ideological wars and revolutions, as well as in religious, political and racial persecutions within a country. In all these cases, delusion produces hate, with greed too often lurking in the background. Oppressive regimes, in their acts directed against sections of their own people, share the same motive. The interaction of the roots is sometimes quite complex, as they grow in strength by feeding each other.

The Buddha understood well the psychology of the mighty, which basically has not changed through the millenia. All those wrongful acts, from killing down to expulsion of innocent victims, are committed out of the lust for power—the enjoyment of power, the wish to secure it and the drive to expand its range. This power craze is, of course, an obsessive delusion intricately bound up with authority. It threatens to overcome all those who exercise authority over others, from the old-style monarchs to the modern dictator. Even the petty bureaucrat does not escape: he too delights in wielding his own little share of power and displaying his stamp of authority.

V. The Removal of the Unwholesome Roots

23. The Triple Gem and the Abandoning of the Evil Roots

Once the venerable Ānanda was staying in Kosambī, at Ghosita's monastery. At that time a certain householder, a lay devotee of the Ājīvaka ascetics, went to see the venerable Ānanda. Having arrived, he saluted him and sat down at one side. So seated, he said this to the venerable Ānanda:

"How is it, revered Ānanda: Whose doctrine is *well-proclaimed*? Who are those who live *well-conducted* in the world? Who are the *blessed ones* in the world?"[1]

"Now, householder, I shall ask you a question on this matter, and you may answer as you think fit. What do you think, householder: as to those who teach a doctrine for the abandoning of greed, hatred and

---

1. The words used here, "well-proclaimed" (*svākkhāta*), "well-conducted" (*supaṭipanna*) and "blessed ones" (*sugata*) are key words in the well-known formula of homage to the Dhamma, Sangha and the Buddha (in our text, in this sequence). The term *sugata*, "well-farer," was perhaps pre-Buddhist usage for a saintly person and was later on increasingly applied to the Buddha as one of his epithets. In Medieval India, the Buddhists were known as *Saugata*, the followers of the Sugata.

The Removal of the Unwholesome Roots

delusion, is their doctrine well-proclaimed or not? Or what do you think about this?"

"I think their doctrine is well-proclaimed, revered sir."

"Then, householder, what do you think: those whose conduct is directed to the abandoning of greed, hatred and delusion, do they live well-conducted in this world or not? Or what do you think about this?"

"I think they are well-conducted, revered sir."

"And further, householder, what do you think: those in whom greed, hatred and delusion are abandoned, cut off at the root, made (barren) like a palm-stump, brought to non-existence, no longer liable to arise in the future again—are they the blessed ones in the world or not? Or what do you think about this?"

"Yes, I do think, revered sir, that these are the blessed ones in the world."

"So, householder, you have admitted this: Well-proclaimed is the creed of those who teach a doctrine for the abandoning of greed, hatred and delusion. Those are well-conducted whose conduct is directed to the abandoning of greed, hatred and delusion. And the blessed ones are those who have abandoned greed, hatred and delusion and have totally destroyed it in themselves."

"Wonderful, revered sir! Marvellous, revered sir! There was no extolling of your creed, nor a disparaging of another's creed. Just by keeping to the subject matter, the doctrine was explained by you. Only facts were spoken of and no selfish reference was brought in.

"It is excellent, revered sir, very excellent. It is as if one were to set aright what was overturned, reveal what was hidden, point the way to those who have lost it, hold up a light in the darkness so that those who have eyes may see what is visible. Thus was the teaching in diverse ways explained by the worthy Ānanda.

"I now go for refuge to that Exalted One, to his Teaching, and to the Order of monks. May master Ānanda accept me as a lay follower from this day onwards as long as life shall last. May he regard me as one who has thus taken refuge."

AN 3:71

Comment

This text introduces us to an unnamed lay follower of the Ājīvakas, a sect of naked ascetics contemporary with the Buddha. The questioner must have been a person of sensitivity, and was obviously disgusted with the self-advertisement he may have found in his own sect and among other contemporary religious teachers. So he wanted to test a disciple of the Buddha to see if they too indulged in self-praise. He even laid a trap for the venerable Ānanda, by phrasing his questions in terms of the well-known Buddhist formula of homage to the Triple Gem. Perhaps he expected that the venerable Ānanda would answer thus: "These are the very words we use, and we claim these achievements for our doctrine, for our monks and for our Buddha." But the venerable Ānanda's reply, being free from self-praise and blame of others, came as a happy surprise to him. And as the questioner was perceptive, he immediately grasped the profound significance of the venerable Ānanda's words connecting the Three Gems with the abandonment of the unwholesome roots. Moved to admiration for both the speaker and his teaching, the inquirer declared on the spot his dedication to the Triple Gem.

This dialogue between a non-Buddhist and a Buddhist monk suggests that the teaching on the three roots can be immediately convincing to anyone with an open mind and heart. It offers an eminently practical, non-creedal approach to the very core of the Dhamma, even for those reluctant to accept its other tenets. It is for this reason that the awareness of those three roots and their significance is elsewhere called a directly "visible teaching" (Text 20) and a doctrine that can be grasped without recourse to faith, tradition or ideologies (Text 33). It can be easily seen that greed, hatred and delusion are at the root of all individual and social conflict. Those who still hesitate to accept the Buddha's teaching on the truths of suffering and its origin in their entire range of validity may not be ready to admit that *all* degrees and varieties of greed, hatred and delusion are roots of suffering. Yet even if they only understand the more extreme forms of those three states to be the root causes of evil and unhappiness, such understanding, practically applied, will be immensely beneficial to themselves and to society.

From such an initial understanding and application, it may not be too difficult for an honest searching mind to proceed to the conclusion that even the very subtle tendencies towards greed, hatred and delusion are harmful—seeds from which their most destructive forms may grow. But the Dhamma is a gradual teaching: the extension of that initial understanding should be left to the natural growth of the individual's own insight and experience without being forced upon him. This was the very attitude which the Enlightened One himself observed in his way of teaching.

Following the example of the venerable Ānanda, it will be profitable also in the present day if, for various levels of understanding, the practical message of the Dhamma is formulated in terms of the wholesome and unwholesome roots. In its simplicity as well as its profundity, this teaching carries the distinct seal of Enlightenment. It is a teaching that will directly affect everyday life, and will also reach to the very depth of existence, showing the way to transcend all suffering.

24. The Purpose of the Teaching

Sīha, a general and formerly a disciple of the Nigaṇṭhas (Jains), once questioned the Buddha about various accusations levelled against him. One of them was that the Buddha taught a destructive doctrine and was a nihilist, a destroyer. The Buddha replied:

"There is one way, Sīha, in which one might rightly speak of me as a destroyer, as one who teaches his doctrine with a destructive purpose: because I teach Dhamma for the purpose of destroying greed, hatred and delusion; for the destroying of manifold evil and unwholesome states of mind do I teach Dhamma."

Aṅguttara Nikāya, 3:12

25. It Can Be Done

Abandon what is unwholesome, O monks! One *can* abandon the unwholesome, O monks! If it were not possible, I would not ask you to do so.

If this abandoning of the unwholesome would bring harm and suffering, I would not ask you to abandon it. But as the abandoning of the unwholesome brings benefit and happiness, therefore I say, "Abandon what is unwholesome!"

Cultivate what is wholesome, O monks! One *can* cultivate the wholesome, O monks! If it were not possible, I would not ask you to do so.

If this cultivation of the wholesome would bring harm and suffering, I would not ask you to cultivate it. But as the cultivation of the wholesome brings benefit and happiness, therefore I say, "Cultivate what is wholesome!"

AN 2:19

Comment

This text proclaims, in simple and memorable words, man's potential for achieving the good, thus invalidating the common charge that Buddhism is pessimistic. But since man also has, as we know only too well, a strong potential for evil, there is as little ground for unreserved optimism about him and his future. Which of his potentialities becomes actual—that for good or that for evil—depends on his own choice. What makes a person a full human being is facing choices and making use of them. The range of man's choices and his prior awareness of them expand with the growth of his mindfulness and wisdom, and as mindfulness and wisdom grow, those forces that seem to "condition" and even to compel his choices into a wrong direction become weakened.

These hope-inspiring words of the Buddha about man's positive potential will be grasped in their tremendous significance and their full range if we remember that the words wholesome and unwholesome are not limited to a narrow moral application. The wholesome that can be cultivated comprises everything beneficial, including those qualities of mind and heart which are indispensable for reaching the highest goal of final liberation. The unwholesome that can be abandoned includes even the finest traces of greed, hatred and delusion. It is, indeed, a bold and heartening assurance—a veritable "lion's roar"—when the Buddha said, with such wide implications, that what is beneficial can be cultivated and what is harmful can be abandoned.

26. The Arising and Non-Arising of the Roots

There may be outsiders, O monks, who will ask you:

"Now, friends, what is the cause and condition whereby unarisen greed arises and arisen greed becomes stronger and more powerful?" "An attractive object," they should be told. In him who gives unwise attention to an attractive object, unarisen greed will arise, and greed that has already arisen will become stronger and more powerful.

"Now, friends, what is the cause and condition whereby unarisen hatred arises and arisen hatred becomes stronger and more powerful?" "A repulsive object," they should be told. In him who gives unwise attention to a repulsive object, unarisen hatred will arise, and hatred that has already arisen will grow stronger and more powerful.

"Now, friends, what is the cause and condition whereby unarisen delusion arises and arisen delusion becomes stronger and more powerful?" "Unwise attention," they should be told. In him who gives unwise attention, unarisen delusion will arise, and delusion that has already arisen will grow stronger and more powerful.

"Now, friends, what is the cause and condition for unarisen greed not to arise and for the abandoning of greed that has arisen?" "A (meditation) object of impurity," they should be told. In him who gives wise attention to a (meditation) object of impurity, unarisen greed will not arise and greed that has arisen will be abandoned.

"Now, friends, what is the cause and condition for unarisen hatred not to arise and for the abandoning of hatred that has arisen?" "Loving-kindness that is a freeing of the mind," they should be told. In him who gives wise attention to loving kindness that is a freeing of the mind, unarisen hatred will not arise and hatred that has arisen will be abandoned.

"Now, friends, what is the cause and condition for unarisen delusion not to arise and for the abandoning of delusion that has arisen?" "Wise attention," they should be told. In him who gives wise attention, unarisen delusion will not arise and delusion that has arisen will be abandoned.

AN 3:68

Comment

This text shows the decisive role attention plays in the origination and eradication of the unwholesome roots. In the discourse "All Taints" (Sabbāsava Sutta, MN 2) it is said: "The uninstructed common man ... does not know the things worthy of attention nor those unworthy of attention. Hence he fails to give attention to what is worthy of it and directs his attention to what is unworthy of it." And of the well-instructed disciple the same discourse says that he knows what is worthy of attention and what is not, and that he acts accordingly.

The commentary to that discourse makes a very illuminating remark: "There is nothing definite in the nature of the things (or objects) themselves that makes them worthy or unworthy of attention; but there is such definiteness in the *manner* (*ākāra*) of attention. A manner of attention that provides a basis for the arising of what is unwholesome or evil (*akusala*), that kind of attention should not be given (to the respective object); but the kind of attention that is the basis for the arising of the good and wholesome (*kusala*), that manner of attention should be given."

It is this latter type of attention that in our present text is called "wise attention" (*yoniso manasikāra*). The former kind is "unwise attention" (*ayoniso manasikāra*), which elsewhere in the commentaries is said to be the proximate cause of delusion.

Things pleasant or unpleasant—that is, those potentially attractive or repulsive—are given to us as facts of common experience, but there is nothing compelling in their own nature that determines our reaction to them. It is our own deliberate attitude towards them, the "manner of attention," which decides whether we will react with greed to the pleasant and with aversion to the unpleasant, or whether our attention will be governed instead by right mindfulness and right understanding, resulting in right action. In some cases, it will also be possible and advisable to withdraw or divert attention altogether from an object; and this is one of the methods recommended by the Buddha for the removal of unwholesome thoughts. (See

Text 27 and Comment.)

Our freedom of choice is present in our very first reaction to a given experience, that is, in the way we attend to it. But only if we direct *wise* attention to the object perceived can we make use of our potential freedom of choice for our own true benefit. The range of freedom can be further widened if we train ourselves to raise that wise attention to the level of right mindfulness.

27. Five Methods for Removing Unwholesome Thoughts

A monk who is intent on the higher consciousness (of meditation) should from time to time give attention to five items. What five?

1. When, owing to an object to which the monk has given (wrong) attention, there arise in him evil unwholesome thoughts connected with desire,[1] with hatred and with delusion, then that monk should give his attention to a different object, to one connected with what is wholesome. When he is doing so, those evil unwholesome thoughts connected with desire, hatred and delusion are abandoned in him and subside. With their abandonment, his mind becomes inwardly steady and settled, unified and concentrated....

2. If, when giving attention to an object that is wholesome, there still arise in him evil unwholesome

---

1. Here, the Pali term used is *chanda*, not *rāga* (lust) or *lobha* (greed).

thoughts connected with desire, with hatred and with delusion, then the monk should reflect upon the danger in these thoughts thus: "Truly, for such and such reasons these thoughts are unwholesome, they are reprehensible and result in suffering!" When he is reflecting in this way, those evil unwholesome thoughts are abandoned in him and subside. With their abandonment, his mind becomes inwardly steady and settled, unified and concentrated....

3. If, when reflecting upon the danger in these thoughts, there still arise in him evil unwholesome thoughts connected with desire, with hatred and with delusion, he should try not to be mindful of them, not to give attention to them. When he is not giving attention to them, those evil unwholesome thoughts will be abandoned in him and subside. With their abandonment, his mind becomes inwardly steady and settled, unified and concentrated....

4. If, when he is not giving attention to these thoughts, there still arise in him evil unwholesome thoughts connected with desire, with hatred and with delusion, he should give attention to the removal of the source of these thoughts.[1] When he is doing so, those evil unwholesome thoughts are abandoned in him and subside. With their abandonment, his mind becomes inwardly steady and settled, unified and concentrated....

---

1. This rendering follows the sutta's commentary which explains the word *saṅkhāra* (in the phrase *vitakka-saṅkhāra-saṇṭhāna*) by condition, cause or root. An alternative rendering of this phrase would be "quieting the thought formations."

5. If, while he is giving attention to the removal of the source of these thoughts, these evil unwholesome thoughts still arise in him, he should, with teeth clenched and the tongue pressed against the palate, restrain, subdue and suppress mind by mind.[1] When he is doing so, those evil unwholesome thoughts are abandoned in him and subside. With their abandonment, his mind becomes inwardly steady and settled, unified and concentrated....

When those evil unwholesome thoughts connected with desire, hate and delusion, which have arisen owing to (wrong) attention given to an object, have been abandoned in a monk and have subsided (due to his applying these five methods), and when (due to that) his mind has become steady and settled, unified and concentrated—then that monk is called a master of the pathways of thoughts: he will think the thoughts he wants to think and will not think those he does not want to think. He has cut off craving, severed the fetter (to existence) and with the full penetration of conceit, he has made an end of suffering.

MN 20 (Vitakkasaṇṭhāna Sutta)[2]

---

1. That is, he has to restrain the unwholesome state of mind by a wholesome state of mind, i.e., by his efforts to remove those unwholesome thoughts.

2. For a complete translation, including the commentary, see *The Removal of Distracting Thoughts*, tr. by Soma Thera (Wheel No. 21).

Comment

This Discourse on the Removal of Unwholesome Thoughts was addressed by the Buddha to monks devoted to meditation, especially to the attainment of the meditative absorptions (*jhāna*), which constitute the higher consciousness (*adhicitta*) mentioned in the sutta. But the five methods for stopping unwholesome thoughts are not restricted to those engaged in strict meditative practice. They are also helpful when desire, aversion and delusion arise during less intensive contemplations undertaken by monks or lay people. Even in situations of ordinary life, when one is confronted with an onrush of unwholesome thoughts, these methods will prove effective, provided one can muster the presence of mind needed to promptly apply them. In applying them, one will be practising right effort, the sixth factor of the Noble Eightfold Path. For the attempt to overcome arisen unwholesome thoughts is one of the four great efforts (*sammappadhāna*), constituting the path factor of right effort.

By the *first* method one tries to replace harmful thoughts by their beneficial opposites. The discourse gives the simile of a carpenter removing a coarse peg with the help of a fine peg. The commentary explains as follows: when an unwholesome thought of desire for a living being arises, one should counter it by thinking of the impurity of the body; if there is desire for an inanimate object, one should consider its impermanence and its ownerless nature. In the case of aversion against a living being, one should direct thoughts of loving kindness and friendliness towards that being; one should remove resentment against inanimate things or against adverse situations by thinking of their impermanence and impersonal nature. When deluded or confused thoughts arise, one should make an effort to clarify them and discern things as they are.

The sutta statement deals with the case of countering undesirable thoughts immediately on their arising. For sustained success in substantially reducing and finally abolishing them, one should strengthen the wholesome roots opposed to them whenever one meets the opportunity to do so. Non-greed should be enhanced by selflessness, generosity and acts of renunciation; non-hate by patience and compassion; non-delusion by cultivating clarity of thought and a penetrative understanding of reality.

The *second* method for removing unwholesome thoughts is that of evoking repugnance and a sense of danger with regard to them. The simile in the discourse is that of a well-dressed young man or woman who feels horrified, humiliated and disgusted when the carcass of an animal is slung around his or her neck. Calling to mind the unworthiness of evil thoughts will produce a sense of shame (*hiri*) and abhorrence. The awareness that these unwholesome thoughts are harmful and dangerous will produce a deterring "dread of consequences" (*ottappa*). This method of evoking repugnance may also serve as an aid for returning to the first method of "replacement by good thoughts," unless one has now become able to check the intruding thoughts through the second method. This method can be very effective when encounters in ordinary life call for quick restraint of the mind.

By the *third* method one tries to ignore undesirable thoughts by diverting one's attention to other thoughts or activities. Here the simile is that of closing one's eyes at a disagreeable sight or looking in another direction. If this method is applied during a session of meditation, it may require a temporary interruption of the meditation. For a diverting occupation, the commentary gives as examples recitation, reading or looking through the contents of one's bag (or pocket). Reciting or reading may be helpful outside meditative practice, too. Until those troublesome thoughts have subsided, one might also take up some little work that requires attention.

The *fourth* method is illustrated in the discourse by a man who runs fast and then asks himself: "Why should I run?" and he slows down; he then continues that process of calming his activity by successively standing still, sitting and lying down. This simile suggests that this method involves a sublimating and refining of the coarse unwholesome thoughts. But as this sublimation is a slow and gradual process, it may not be applicable to a meditative situation when a quicker remedial action is required. The commentarial interpretation seems, therefore, to be preferable: one traces unwholesome thoughts back to the thoughts or the situation which caused them to arise and then tries to remove that thought source from one's mind. This may often be easier than confronting directly the full-grown end-result. It will also help to divert the mind (according to the third method) from those unwholesome thoughts, which at this stage may be hard to dislodge. We may thus describe the fourth method as "tracing the thought source." But from the longer view of a continued endeavour to eliminate the harmful thoughts, interpreting this method as sublimation and gradual refinement need not be excluded. Such refinement can reduce the intensity and the immoral quality of the three unwholesome roots and even divert their energy into wholesome channels.

The *fifth* and last method is that of vigorous suppression. This method is to be applied when unwholesome thoughts have gained such a strength that they threaten to become unmanageable and to bring about situations of grave peril, practically and morally. The discourse illustrates this method by a strong-bodied man forcing down a weaker person by sheer physical strength.

If the application of these five methods is not neglected but is kept alive in meditative practice as well as in ordinary circumstances, one can expect a marked and progressive weakening of the three unwholesome roots, culminating in the perfect mastery of thoughts promised at the end of the sutta.

28. For One's Own Sake

For one's own sake, monks, vigilant mindfulness should be made the mind's guard and this for four reasons:

"May my mind not harbour lust for anything inducing lust!"—for this reason vigilant mindfulness should be made the mind's guard, for one's own sake.

"May my mind not harbour hatred toward anything inducing hatred!"—for this reason vigilant mindfulness should be made the mind's guard, for one's own sake.

"May my mind not harbour delusion concerning anything inducing delusion!"—for this reason vigilant mindfulness should be made the mind's guard, for one's own sake.

"May my mind not be infatuated by anything inducing infatuation!"—for this reason vigilant mindfulness should be made the mind's guard, for one's own sake.

When now, monks, a monk's mind does not harbour lust for lust-inducing things, because he is free from lust;

when his mind does not harbour hatred toward hate-inducing things, because he is free from hatred;

when his mind does not harbour delusion concerning anything inducing delusion, because he is free from delusion;

when his mind is not infatuated by anything inducing infatuation, because he is free from infatuation—then such a monk will not waver, shake or tremble, he will not succumb to fear, nor will he adopt the views of other recluses.[1]

AN 4:17

---

1. That is, other religious or philosophical ideas.

29. The Noble Power

Monks, it is good for a monk if, from time to time:

he perceives the repulsive in the unrepulsive,

if he perceives the unrepulsive in the repulsive,

if he perceives the repulsive in both the unrepulsive and the repulsive,

if he perceives the unrepulsive in both the repulsive and the unrepulsive,

if he avoids both the repulsive and the unrepulsive (aspects), and dwells in equanimity, mindful and clearly comprehending.

But with what motive should a monk perceive the repulsive in the unrepulsive? "May no lust arise in me for lust-inducing objects!"—it is with such a motive that he should perceive in this way.

With what motive should he perceive the unrepulsive in the repulsive? "May no hatred arise in me towards hate-inducing objects!"—it is with such a motive that he should perceive in this way.

With what motive should he perceive the repulsive in the unrepulsive as well as in the repulsive? "May no lust arise in me for lust-inducing objects nor hatred towards hate-inducing objects!"—it is with such a motive that he should perceive in this way.

With what motive should he perceive the unrepulsive in the repulsive as well as in the unrepulsive? "May no hatred arise in me towards lust-inducing objects nor lust for lust-inducing objects!"—it is with such a motive that he should perceive in this way.

The Removal of the Unwholesome Roots

With what motive should he avoid both the repulsive and the unrepulsive, and dwell in equanimity, mindful and clearly comprehending? "May lust for lust-inducing objects, hatred towards hate-inducing objects, and delusion towards deluding objects never arise in me anywhere in any way!"—it is with such a motive that he should avoid both the repulsive and the unrepulsive, and dwell in equanimity, mindful and clearly comprehending.

AN 5:144

Comment

This fivefold method of mastering perception is called in Pali *ariya-iddhi*, a term which may be rendered as noble power, noble success or noble magic; or, alternatively, as the power, success or magic of the noble ones (*ariya*). In its perfection, this arduous practice can be ascribed only to Arahants, as several suttas and commentaries indicate. But, as our text shows at the beginning, the Buddha recommended this training to the monks in general, including those in whom the three unwholesome roots were still active. It is eradication of these roots that is said to be the motivation for taking up this practice.

For applying this fivefold power, the following directions have been given in the Canon and commentaries.[1]

---

1. Compiled from the Paṭisambhidāmagga and commentaries to the Dīgha Nikāya and Aṅguttara Nikāya.

1. To perceive the repulsive in the unrepulsive, one pervades attractive living beings with the contemplation of the body's impurity; towards attractive inanimate objects one applies the contemplation of impermanence.

2. To perceive the unrepulsive in the repulsive, one pervades repulsive living beings with loving kindness and views repulsive inanimate objects as consisting of the four elements; but living beings too ought to be contemplated by way of the elements.

3. To perceive the repulsive in both the unrepulsive and the repulsive, one pervades both with the contemplation of impurity and applies to them the contemplation of impermanence. Or, if one has first judged a being to be attractive and later repulsive, one now regards it as unrepulsive throughout, i.e., from the viewpoint of impurity and impermanence.[1]

4. To perceive the unrepulsive in both the repulsive and the unrepulsive, one pervades both with loving kindness and views both as bare elements. Or, if one has first judged a being to be repulsive and later attractive, one now regards it as unrepulsive throughout; i.e., from the viewpoint of loving kindness and as consisting of elements.

5. Avoiding both aspects, one applies the six-factored equanimity of which it is said: "On perceiving (any of the six sense objects, including mental objects), he is neither glad nor sad, but keeps to equanimity and

---

[1]. "Owing to a change in one's own attitude towards a person or due to a change in character (or behaviour) of that person." Sub. Comy. to Majjhima Nikāya.

is mindful and clearly comprehending." He does not lust after a desirable object nor does he hate an undesirabe one; and where others thoughtlessly allow delusion to arise, he does not give room to delusion. He remains equanimous towards the six objects, being equipped with the six-factored equanimity which does not abandon the pure natural state of the mind.

These five methods of applying the noble power have several applications. They are first for use during meditation, when images of repulsive and unrepulsive beings or things arise in the mind. At such a time one can overcome the attraction or aversion by dwelling on the counteractive ideas—such as loving kindness or analysis into elements—as long as required to dispel the defilements. Second, these methods can be used in the encounters of everyday life when the counteractive ideas must be tersely formulated and rapidly applied. This will require previous familiarity with them and alertness of mind. In encounters with repulsive people one may also think of their good qualities and of their common human nature, with its failings and sufferings. When meeting a physically attractive person, one may vividly visualize that person's body as subject to ageing and decay.

These five modes of perception, as perfected in the Arahat, reveal the high-point of the mind's sovereign mastery over the world of feelings and emotions. They show a state where the response to provocative objects, usually so habitually fixed, can be chosen at will. This approach differs from that used in the contemplation of feelings as shown below (Text 35). In the latter the feeling-values of experience are accepted as they are given, but by applying bare attention to them, one "stops short" at the feelings themselves without allowing them to grow into the passionate reactions of lust or aversion. However, in this method of the noble power, the meditator does not take the feeling-values for granted; he does not accept them as they present themselves. His response is to reverse the feeling-value (mode 1, 2), to equalize the response to the repulsive and the unrepulsive (mode 3, 4) and to transcend both by mindful equanimity (mode 5).

These fives modes thus constitute a subtle "magic of transformation" by which pleasant and unpleasant feelings, as they habitually arise, can be changed at will or replaced by equanimity. A mind that has gone through this training has passed the most severe test, indeed. Through that training, it obtains an increasing control over emotive reactions, and internal independence from the influence of habits and passions. It is said in the Satipaṭṭhāna Sutta, "He dwells independent and clings to nothing." These words conclude a statement recurring after each of the exercises given in the sutta. In the light of the above observations, it is significant that they also occur after the section on contemplation of feelings found in that sutta.

According to our text, the purpose for cultivating the noble power is the eradication of greed, hatred and delusion. In a mind disciplined in this radical training, the root defilements cannot find a fertile soil for growth. The training also provides the experiential basis for comprehending the true nature of feelings as being relative and subjective. This the five modes of the noble power demonstrate in a convincing way. The relativity of feelings and of the emotions roused by them was succinctly expressed by Āryadeva (2nd century CE):

> By the same thing lust is incited in one, hate in the other, delusion in the next. Hence sense objects have no inherent value.
>
> *Catuḥ-Śataka*, 8:177

Perfection in applying this noble power is the domain only of the truly noble ones, the Arahats, whose mastery of mind and strength of will are equal to the task of exercising it effortlessly. But also on much lower levels, an earnest endeavour to develop this noble power will be of great benefit. In the text here commented upon, the Buddha does not restrict the cultivation of the noble power to Arahats, but begins his exposition with the words: "It is good for a monk...." We may add: not only for a monk. Prior practice of right mindfulness (*satipaṭṭhāna*), however, will be indispensable. Of particular importance is the contemplation of feelings, by which one learns to distinguish between the feeling linked with a perception and the subsequent emotional reaction to it.

30. The Four Ways of Progress

There are four ways of progress: difficult progress with slow understanding, difficult progress with swift understanding, easy progress with slow understanding, and easy progress with swift understanding.*

What is the difficult progress with slow understanding? There is one who naturally has strong greed, strong hatred and strong delusion, and caused by it he often suffers pain and grief. The five faculties, namely faith, energy, mindfulness, concentration and wisdom,** appear in him only in a weak state; and due to their weakness he attains but slowly the immediate condition for the destruction of the taints.***

What is the difficult progress with swift understanding? There is one who naturally has strong greed, strong hatred and strong delusion, and caused by it he often suffers pain and grief. But the five faculties, namely faith, energy, mindfulness, concentration, and wisdom, appear in him in a very strong degree, and due to their strength he attains swiftly the immediate condition for the destruction of the taints.

What is the easy progress with slow understanding? There is one who naturally is without strong greed, strong hatred and strong delusion, and therefore he does not often suffer pain and grief, caused by them. The five faculties, however, appear in him only in a weak state; and due to their weakness he attains only slowly the immediate condition for the destruction of the taints.

What is the easy progress with swift understanding? There is one who naturally is without strong greed, strong hatred and strong delusion, and therefore he does not often suffer pain and grief, caused by them. The five faculties, namely faith, energy, mindfulness, concentration and wisdom, appear in him in a very strong degree; and due to their strength he attains swiftly to the immediate condition for the destruction of the taints.

Aṅguttara Nikāya, 4: 162

Comments

* For the four ways of progress (*catasso paṭipadā*), see *The Path of Purification* (*Visuddhimagga*), pp. 87 ff. In the case of "difficult progress" (*dukkha-paṭipadā*), the term *dukkha* has three different connotations: (1) Difficult, (2) painful due to the presence of strong greed, etc, (3) "unpleasant" if progress is achieved with an unpleasant subject of meditation such as the foulness of the body. In the case of easy progress (*sukha-paṭipadā*), *sukha* refers: (a) to a relatively easy conquest of the passions, which thus do not cause much suffering; (b) to the happiness experienced during the meditative absorptions (*jhāna*), which likewise constitute the happy mode of progress.

** Well-balanced and strongly developed faculties (*indriya*) are the essential mental tools for successful insight meditation (*vipassanā*), culminating in Arahatship. On the faculties, see *The Way of Wisdom* by Edward Conze, *Wheel* No. 65/66.

*** "Immediate condition" (*ānantariyaṃ*), according to the commentary, refers to the concentration of mind associated with the path (of Arahatship; *magga-samādhi*). This concentration, lasting for a single moment, precedes the immediately following attainment to the fruition of Arahatship, where the destruction of the taints (*āsavānaṃ khaya*) reaches its consummation.

VI. Removal through Mindfulness and Insight

31. To Be Abandoned by Seeing

Which are the things, O monks, that can neither be abandoned by bodily acts nor by speech, but can be abandoned by wisely seeing them? Greed can neither be abandoned by bodily acts nor by speech; but it can be abandoned by wisely seeing it. Hatred can neither be abandoned by bodily acts nor by speech; but it can be abandoned by wisely seeing it. Delusion can neither be abandoned by bodily acts nor by speech; but it can be abandoned by wisely seeing it.

AN 10:23

Comment

"Wisely seeing," according to the commentary, refers here to the wisdom pertaining to the paths of emancipation along with the insight that culminates in the paths. From this explanation it follows that the term *abandoning* has to be understood here in its strict sense, as final and total elimination, effected by realization of the paths of emancipation (stream-entry, etc.).

Nevertheless, a weakening of the unwholesome roots can be effected also by body and speech, through curbing more and more their outward manifestations in deeds and words, motivated by greed, hatred and delusion.

The phrase "wisely seeing" may serve to emphasize the crucial importance of mindfully observing the presence or absence of the unwholesome roots within one's own mind flux. This repeated confrontation with them prepares the way to liberating insight.

32. From the Satipaṭṭhāna Sutta

And how, monks, does a monk dwell practising mind-contemplation on the mind?

Herein a monk knows the mind with lust as with lust; the mind without lust as without lust; the mind with hatred as with hatred; the mind without hatred as without hatred; the mind with delusion as with delusion; the mind without delusion as without delusion....

Thus he dwells practising mind-contemplation on the mind, internally, or externally, or both internally and externally. He dwells contemplating the states of origination in the mind, or he dwells contemplating the states of dissolution in the mind, or he dwells contemplating the states of both origination and dissolution in the mind. Or his mindfulness that "there is mind" is established in him to the extent necessary for knowledge and awareness. He dwells detached, clinging to nothing in the world.

MN 10

33. Beyond Faith

"Is there a way, O monks, by which a monk without recourse to faith, to cherished opinions, to tradition, to specious reasoning, or to preference for his preconceived views, may declare the final knowledge (of Arahatship), thus: 'Rebirth has ceased, the holy life has been lived, completed is the task, and nothing remains after this'?

"There is such a way, O monks. And what is it?

"Herein, monks, a monk has seen a form with his eyes, and if greed, hatred and delusion are in him, he knows 'There is in me greed, hatred and delusion'; and if greed, hatred and delusion are absent in him, he knows 'There is no greed, hatred and delusion in me.'

"Further, monks, a monk has heard a sound, smelled an odour, tasted a flavour, felt a tactile sensation or cognized a mental object, and if greed, hatred and delusion are in him, he knows, 'There is in me greed, hatred and delusion'; and if greed, hatred and delusion are absent in him, he knows 'There is no greed, hatred and delusion in me.'

"And if he thus knows, O monks, are these ideas such as to be known by recourse to faith, to cherished opinions, to tradition, to specious reasoning or to preference for one's preconceived views?"

"Certainly not, Lord."

"Are these not rather ideas to be known after wisely realizing them by experience?"

"That is so, Lord."

"This, monks, is a way by which a monk, without recourse to faith, to cherished opinions, to tradition, to specious reasoning or to preference for his preconceived views, may declare final knowledge (of Arahatship), thus: 'Rebirth has ceased, the holy life has been lived, completed is the task and nothing more remains after this.'"

SN 35:153

34. The Visible Teaching [1]

Once the venerable Upavāna went to the Exalted One, saluted him respectfully and sat down at one side. Thus seated he addressed the Exalted One as follows:

"People speak of the 'visible teaching.' In how far, Lord, is the teaching visible here and now, of immediate result, inviting to come and see, onward-leading, to be directly experienced by the wise?"

"Herein, Upavāna, a monk, having seen a form with his eyes, experiences the form and experiences desire for the form.[2] Of the desire for forms present in him, he knows: 'There is in me a desire for forms.' If a monk, having seen a form with his eyes, experiencing the form

───────────────
1. See also Text 20.

and experiencing desire for the form, knows that desire for forms is present in him—in so far, Upavāna, is the teaching visible here and now, of immediate result, inviting to come and see, onward-leading, to be directly experienced by the wise.

"It is similar if a monk experiences desire when he hears a sound with his ears, smells an odour with his nose, tastes a flavour with his tongue, feels a tangible with his body or cognizes an idea with his mind. If he knows in each case that desire is present in him—in so far, Upavāna, is the teaching visible here and now, of immediate result, inviting to come and see, onward-leading, to be directly experienced by the wise.

"Further, Upavāna, a monk, having seen a form with his eyes, experiences the form without experiencing desire for the form. Of the absent desire for form he knows: 'There is in me no desire for forms.' If a monk, having seen a form with his eyes, experiencing the form without experiencing desire for the form, knows that desire for forms is not present in him—in so far, too, Upavāna, is the teaching visible here and now, of immediate result, inviting to come and see, onward-leading, to be directly experienced by the wise.

"It is similar if a monk does not experience desire when he hears a sound with his ears, smells an odour with his nose, tastes a flavour with his tongue, feels a tangible with his body or cognizes an idea with his

---

2. Though this text refers only to desire (*rāga,* "lust"), the statements in it are also valid for a reaction to the six-fold sense perception by hatred and delusion.

mind. If he knows in each case that desire is not present in him—in so far, Upavāna, is the teaching visible here and now, of immediate result, inviting to come and see, onward-leading, to be directly experienced by the wise."

SN 35:70

Comment on Texts 32–34

When thoughts connected with greed (desire, attraction), hatred (anger, aversion) or delusion (prejudices, false views) arise in an untrained mind, generally one reacts to them in one of two ways: either one allows oneself to be carried away by them or one tries to repress them. The first type of reaction is a full identification with the unwholesome roots; the second extreme is the attempt to ignore their presence, shirking a confrontation with them. In this latter case, one regards the defiled thoughts as a disreputable part of one's mind, harmful to one's self-esteem, and thus blots them out from one's awareness.

The approach through *bare attention*, as indicated in the above texts, is a middle way that avoids these two extremes. It involves neither passive submission nor anxious recoil, but a full awareness of the unwholesome thoughts while holding to the mental post of detached observation. These thoughts will then be seen simply as psychological events, as impersonal and conditioned mental processes, as "mere phenomena rolling on" (*suddhadhammā pavattanti*). When thus objectified, they will no longer initiate emotional reactions by way of attachment, aversion or fear. Bare attention empties these thoughts of self-reference, and prevents the identification with them as a fictive ego. Thus the confrontation even with one's imperfections may give rise to a clear realization of egolessness. From that, again, there may emerge the state of mind described in the Satipaṭṭhāna Sutta: "He dwells detached, clinging to nothing." It will now be understood why, in Texts 32 and 34, it is said that even the awareness of the unwholesome in oneself can make the teaching "visible here and now."

This application of detached awareness can be said to belong to the first method of Text 27, replacing the arisen unwholesome thoughts by the wholesome ones of right mindfulness. Even if one does not fully succeed with this method, a sober, factual awareness of the inherent danger, according to the second method, may prove to be effective. If not, one may then be obliged to use the stronger emotional impact of repugnance to eliminate them.

35. Removal through the Contemplation of Feelings

In the case of pleasant feelings, O monks, the underlying tendency to lust should be given up; in the case of painful feelings the underlying tendency to resistance (aversion) should be given up; in the case of neutral feelings, the underlying tendency to ignorance should be given up.

If a monk has given up the tendency to lust in regard to pleasant feelings, the tendency to resistance in regard to painful feelings, and the tendency to ignorance in regard to neutral feelings, then he is called one who is free of unwholesome tendencies, one who has the right outlook. He has cut off craving, severed the fetter to existence, and, through the full penetration of conceit, he has made an end of suffering.[1]

> *If one feels joy, but knows not feeling's nature,*
> *Bent towards greed, one will not find deliverance.*
>
> *If one feels pain, but knows not feeling's nature,*
> *Bent towards hate, one will not find deliverance.*
>
> *And even neutral feeling which as peaceful*
> *The Lord of Wisdom has proclaimed,*
> *If, in attachment, one should cling to it,*
> *One will not be free from the round of ill.*
>
> *But if a monk is ardent and does not neglect*
> *To practise mindfulness and comprehension clear,*
> *The nature of all feelings will he penetrate.*
>
> *And having done so, in this very life*
> *He will be free from cankers and all taints.*
> *Mature in knowledge, firm in Dhamma's ways,*
> *When once his life-span ends, his body breaks,*
> *All measure and concepts he will transcend.*

SN 36:3

---

[1]. "Conceit" refers in particular to "self-conceit" (*asmi-māna*), on both the intellectual and emotional levels.

Comment

In these three "underlying tendencies" (*anusaya*), we encounter the three unwholesome roots under different names. These tendencies are defilements which, by repeated occurrence, have become habitual responses to situations provoking greed, hate and delusion, and hence tend to appear again and again. They may also be called inherent propensities of the mind. Underlying the stream of consciousness in a state of latency, they are always ready to spring up when a stimulus incites them, manifesting themselves as unwholesome deeds, words or thoughts. By having grown into underlying tendencies, the three roots obtain a most tenacious hold on the mind. Even moral conduct (*sīla*) and concentration (*samādhi*), by themselves, cannot prevail against the tendencies; at best they can only check their outward manifestations. To uproot the tendencies at the level of depth, what is required is insight-wisdom (*vipassanā-paññā*), aided by virtue and concentration. The insight-wisdom needed to fully uproot the three must have the strength acquired at the two final stages of emancipation, non-return and Arahatship.[1]

The non-returner eliminates completely the tendency to resistance or aversion, i.e., the root "hatred"; the tendency to lust, i.e., the root "greed," he eliminates as far as it extends to desire for the five outer sense pleasures.

---

1. See *Manual of Insight*, Ledi Sayādaw (Wheel No. 31/32), pp. 81 ff.

The Arahat eliminates the remaining tendency to lust, the desire for fine-material and immaterial existence, and also all tendencies to ignorance, the root "delusion."

Though not able to effect a final elimination of the underlying tendencies, moral restraint in bodily and verbal acts helps to reduce the active formation of *new* unwholesome tendencies, and concentration helps to control the *mental* source of such tendencies, at least temporarily. Insight-wisdom attained on levels lower than the noble paths and fruitions will provide the basis for gradual progress toward the full maturation of liberating wisdom.

The type of insight practice which is particularly efficacious in weakening and removing the underlying tendencies is the Satipaṭṭhāna method called the contemplation of feelings (*vedanānupassanā*). It is the uncontrolled reaction to feelings that produces and nourishes the tendencies. According to Buddhist psychology, the feelings one passively undergoes in sense experience are morally neutral. They are *results* of kamma, not creators of kamma. It is the reaction to feelings following the passive sense encounters that determines the wholesome or unwholesome quality of the responsive active states of consciousness. In the contemplation of feelings, one distinctly realizes that a pleasant feeling is not identical with lust and need not be followed by it; that an unpleasant feeling is not identical with aversion and need not be followed by it; that a neutral feeling is not identical with ignorant, deluded thoughts and need not be followed by them. In that practice, the meditator learns to stop at the bare experience of pleasant, painful and neutral feelings. By doing so, he makes a definite start in cutting through the chain of dependent origination at that decisive point where feeling becomes the condition for craving (*vedanāpaccayā taṇhā*). It will thus become the meditator's indubitable experience that the causal sequence of feeling and craving is not a necessary one, and that the Buddha's words of encouragement are true: "One *can* abandon the unwholesome! If it were not possible, I would not ask you to do so." (See Text 25.)

36. The Dart

An untaught worldling, O monks, experiences a pleasant feeling, he experiences a painful feeling, or he experiences a neutral feeling. A well taught noble disciple likewise experiences a pleasant feeling, a painful feeling at a neutrals feeling. Now, what is the distinction, the diversity, the difference that obtains here between a well-taught noble disciple and an untaught worldling?

When an untaught worldling is touched by a painful feeling, he worries, grieves, and laments, beats his breast, weeps and is distraught. He then experiences two kinds of feelings, a bodily and a mental feeling. It is as if a man were pierced by a dart, and following the first piercing, he is hit by a second dart. So he will experience feelings caused by two darts. It is similar with an untaught worldling: when touched by a painful (bodily) feeling, he worries and grieves; he laments, beats his breast, weeps and is distraught. So he experiences two feelings, a bodily and a mental feeling.

Having been touched by that painful feeling, he resists (and resents) it.[1] Then in him who so resists (and resents) that painful feeling, an underlying tendency of resistance against that painful feeling comes to underlie (his mind).[2] Under the impact of that painful feeling he then proceeds to enjoy sensual happiness. And why does he do so? An untaught worldling, monks does not know of any other escape from painful feelings except the enjoyment of sensual happiness. Then in him who enjoys sensual happiness, an underlying tendency to lust for pleasant feelings comes to underlie (his mind). He does not know, according to facts, the arising and ending of those feelings, nor the gratification, the danger and the escape connected with them. In him who lacks that knowledge, an underlying tendency to ignorance as to neutral feelings comes to underlie (his mind). When he experiences a pleasant feeling or a painful feeling or a neutral feeling, he feels it as one fettered by it. Such a one, O monks, is called an untaught worldling who is fettered by birth, by old age, by death, by sorrow, lamentation, pain, grief and despair. He is fettered to suffering, this I declare.

---

1. *Paṭighavā hoti.*
2. *Paṭighānusayo anuseti*: that is, the underlying tendency manifests itself at that time, and is also strengthened by that manifestation.

Removal through Mindfulness and Insight 85

But in the case of a well-taught noble disciple, O monks, when he is touched by a painful feeling, he does not worry, nor grieve and lament, he does not beat his breast and weep, nor is he distraught. It is one feeling he experiences: a bodily one, but not a mental feeling. It is as if a man were pierced by a dart, but he was not hit by a second dart following the first one. So this person experiences feelings caused by a single dart only. It is similar with a well-taught noble disciple: when touched by a painful feeling, he does not worry, nor grieve and lament, he does not beat his breast and weep, nor is he distraught. He experiences one single feeling, a bodily one.

Having been touched by that painful feeling, he does, not resist (and resent it). Then in him who does not resist (and resent) that painful feeling, no underlying tendency of resistance against that painful feeling comes to underlie (his mind). Hence, under the impact of the painful feeling he does not proceed to enjoy sensual happiness. And why not? As a well-taught noble disciple, he knows of an escape from painful feelings other than the enjoyment of sensual happiness. Then in him who thus does not proceed to enjoy sensual happiness, no underlying tendency to lust for pleasant feeling comes to underlie (his mind). He knows, according to facts, the arising and ending of those feelings' and the gratification, the danger and the escape connected with them. In him who knows thus, no underlying tendency to ignorance as to neutral feelings comes to underlie (his mind). When he experiences a pleasant feeling, or a painful feeling, or a neutral feeling, he feels it as one who is not fettered by it. Such a one, O monks, is called a well-taught noble disciple who is not fettered by birth, by old age, by death; not fettered by sorrow, lamentation, pain, grief and despair. He is not fettered to suffering, this I declare.

This, O monks, is the distinction, the diversity, the difference that obtains between a well-taught noble disciple and an untaught worldling.

Saṃyutta Nikāya, 36:6

37. The Elimination of the Tendencies Arising from Sixfold Sense Perception

Dependent on eye and forms, eye-consciousness arises; dependent on ear and sounds, ear-consciousness arises; dependent on nose and smells, nose-consciousness arises; dependent on tongue and flavours, tongue consciousness arises; dependent on body and tangibles, body-consciousness arises; dependent on mind and mental objects, mind-consciousness arises.

The meeting of the three is contact, and with contact as condition there arises what is felt as pleasant or painful or neutral. If, when touched by pleasant feeling, one does not enjoy it or affirm or accept it, then no underlying tendency to lust any longer underlies it. If, when touched by painful feeling, one does not worry, grieve and lament, does not beat one's breast and weep, and is not distraught, then no underlying tendency to resistance any longer underlies it. If, when touched by a neutral feeling, one understands, according to facts, the arising and ending of that feeling, and the gratification, danger and escape (connected with it), then no underlying tendency to ignorance any longer underlies it. Then, indeed, O monks, that one shall here and now make an end of suffering by abandoning the underlying tendency to lust for pleasant feelings, by eliminating the underlying tendency to resistance against painful feelings, and by abolishing the underlying tendency to ignorance in the case of natural feelings, having thus given up ignorance and produced true knowledge— this is possible.

From Majjhima Nikāya 148, Chachaka Sutta

38. Non-returning

If you give up three things, O monks, I vouchsafe you the state of non-returning. What are these three things? They are greed, hatred and delusion.

> *The greed infatuated by which*
> *beings go to evil destiny,*
> *those of insight give it up*
> *because they fully understand that greed;*
> *and having thus discarded it,*
> *they never return to this world.*

The hate enraged by which
beings go to evil destiny,
those of insight give it up
because they fully understand that hate;
and having thus discarded it,
they never return to this world.

The delusion blinded by which
beings go to evil destiny,
those of insight give it up,
because they fully understand delusion;
and having thus discarded it,
they never return to this world.

Condensed from Itivuttaka 1–3

VII. The Goal

39. The Visible Nibbāna

When greed, hatred and delusion are abandoned, one neither aims at one's own harm, nor at the harm of others, nor at the harm of both, and one will not suffer pain and grief in one's mind. In that sense is Nibbāna visible here and now.

If one experiences the complete elimination of greed, the complete elimination of hatred, the complete elimination of delusion, in that sense is Nibbāna visible here and now, of immediate result, inviting to come and see, onward-leading, to be directly experienced by the wise.

AN 3:56

40. What Is Nibbāna?

A wandering ascetic, Jambukhādaka by name, approached the venerable Sāriputta and asked him the following question:

"One speaks about 'Nibbāna.' Now, what is that Nibbāna, friend?"

"It is the elimination of greed, the elimination of hatred, the elimination of delusion—this, friend, is called Nibbāna."

"But is there a way, is there a path, friend, for the realization of that Nibbāna?"

"Yes, friend, there is such a way, there is a path for the realization of that Nibbāna. It is the Noble Eightfold Path, namely right understanding, right thought, right speech, right action, right livelihood, right effort, right mindfulness and right concentration."

SN 38:1

41. Two Aspects of Nibbāna

This was said by the Blessed One, spoken by the Holy One, and thus I have heard:

There are, O monks, two aspects of Nibbāna: the Nibbāna-element with the groups of existence still remaining (*sa-upādisesa-nibbānadhātu*), and the Nibbāna-element with no groups remaining (*anupādisesa-nibbānadhātu*).

What now is the Nibbāna-element with the groups of existence still remaining? In that case, O monks, a monk is an Arahat: he is taint-free, has fulfilled the holy life, accomplished his task, thrown off the burden, attained his goal, cast off the fetters of existence and is liberated through right wisdom. But there still remain with him (until his death) the five sense-organs that have not yet disappeared and through which he still experiences what is pleasant and unpleasant, as well as bodily ease and pain. The extinction of greed, hatred and delusion in him, this is called the Nibbāna-element with the groups of existence still remaining.

And what is the Nibbāna-element with no groups of existence remaining? In that case, O monks, a monk is an Arahat ... liberated through right wisdom. In him, all those feelings, no longer relished, will even here (at his death) come to extinction. This is called the Nibbāna-element with no groups of existence remaining.

It 44
(Adapted from the translation by
Ñāṇatiloka Mahāthera)

42. *The Happiness of Liberation*

He, the Arahat, knows this:

"Once there was greed, and that was evil; now that is no more, and so it is well. Once there was hatred, and that was evil; now that is no more, and so it is well. Once there was delusion, and that was evil; now that is no more, and so it is well."

Thus the Arahat lives, even during his lifetime, free of craving's hunger, stilled and cooled (of passion's heat), feeling happy, with his heart become holy.

AN 3: 66

VIII. The Roots in the Abhidhamma

In the *Dhammasaṅgaṇī*, the first book of the Abhidhamma Piṭaka, the three unwholesome roots are used for a classification of unwholesome consciousness into twelve classes: eight "rooted in greed" (*lobha-mūla*), two "rooted in hatred" (*dosa-mūla*) and two "rooted in delusion" (*moha-mūla*). These names for the three divisions of unwholesome consciousness are used in the *Visuddhimagga*.[1] The names do not occur in the *Dhammasaṅgaṇī* itself, but the roots are clearly implied. Consciousness rooted in hate is described there as "associated with resentment" (or resistance, *paṭigha-sampayutta*).

The states of consciousness rooted in greed and hatred have delusion as a second root. Delusion, however, can also appear as a single root, without the presence of greed or hatred.

Both the good and the evil roots also occur, of course, in the lists of the mental concomitants (*cetasika*) of wholesome and unwholesome consciousness, respectively.

The wholesome roots, under the name of *hetu*, "root cause," serve also for a classification of rebirth consciousness.

---

1. In the medieval Abhidhamma manuals such as the *Abhidhammatthasaṅgaha*, the nomenclature is: *lobha-sahagata* (accompanied by greed), *paṭigha-sampayutta* (associated with resentment) and *momūha* (strongly delusive).

Rebirth as a human being is always the result of good kamma (*kusala-vipāka*). As rebirth consciousness is a resultant of kamma, and not kamma in itself, the root causes accompanying it are "kammically indeterminate" (*abyākata-hetu*). In human rebirth consciousness, there may be either three accompanying root causes (*ti-hetuka-paṭisandhi*), or when lacking non-delusion, two (*dvi-hetuka-paṭisandhi*) or, in rare cases, none (*ahetuka-paṭisandhi*). In three-rooted rebirth, the strength or weakness of the roots may differ widely. In two-rooted rebirth, the absence of non-delusion, of course, does not mean the entire absence of intelligence, but a complete inability to understand reality and, especially, the Four Noble Truths. Rootless rebirth (*ahetuka-paṭisandhi*) occurs throughout the four lower worlds of misery (animals, ghosts, demons and hellish beings); among humans it is restricted to those born blind, deaf, crippled, mentally deficient, etc.

In almost every human being there is some potential for the good, as human rebirth is always the result of wholesome kamma. We said "almost," because for mentally deficient human beings this potential is greatly handicapped; but not necessarily so for other humans reborn without wholesome root causes (*ahetuka*), as for instance those born crippled, etc. Whether that potential for good is activated and strengthened, or weakened and even lost, depends to a great extent on the type of roots prevailing in the rebirth-producing kamma of the previous life. For this has a strong formative influence on the character tendencies of the present existence, as the following commentarial text will show.

43. The Exposition of Prevalence

In some beings greed is prevalent, in others hatred or delusion; and again in others, non-greed, non-hatred or non-delusion are prevalent. What is it that governs this prevalence? It is the root-cause in the previous life that governs the prevalence of roots in the present life.

There is differentiation at the very moment of the accumulating of kamma. In one person, at the moment of (rebirth-producing) kamma-accumulation, greed is strong and non-greed is weak, non-hatred and non-delusion are strong and hatred and delusion are weak; then his weak non-greed is unable to prevail over his greed, but non-hatred and non-delusion being strong, can prevail over his hatred and delusion. Hence when a being is born through rebirth-linking caused by that kamma, he will be greedy, good-natured, not irascible, intelligent and having knowledge that can be likened to a lightning flash.

In another case, at the moment of kamma-accumulation, greed and hatred are strong, and non-greed and non-hatred are weak, but non-delusion is strong and delusion weak; then, in the way stated, that person will have both greed and hatred, but he will be intelligent and have flash-like knowledge like the Elder Dattābhaya.

When, at the moment of kamma-accumulation, greed, non-hatred and delusion are strong and the other roots are weak, then, in the way stated, that person will be greedy and dull-witted, but he will be good-natured and not irascible.

When, at the moment of kamma-accumulation, the three roots, greed, hatred and delusion are strong and non-greed, etc., are weak, then, in the way stated, that person will be greedy, given to hatred and given to delusion.

When, at the moment of kamma-accumulation, non-greed, hatred and delusion are strong and the others are weak, then, in the way stated, that person will have few (lustful) defilements, being unmoved even when seeing a heavenly sense-object; but he will be given to hatred and his understanding will be slow.

When, at the moment of kamma-accumulation, non-greed, non-hatred and delusion are strong, and the others weak, then, in the way stated, that person will not be greedy and will be good-natured, but he will be slow of understanding.

When, at the moment of kamma-accumulation, non-greed, hatred and non-delusion are strong, and the others weak, then, in the way stated, that person will not be greedy; he will be intelligent, but given to hatred and irascibility.

But when, at the moment of kamma-accumulation, the three (wholesome roots), non-greed, non-hatred and non-delusion are strong, and greed, etc., are weak, then, in the way stated, he has no greed and no hate and he is wise, like the Elder Saṅgharakkhita.

From the *Atthasālinī*, pp. 267f.

44. Root-Cause Condition (hetu-paccaya)

The roots of good and evil are also the constituents of the root-cause condition, or root-cause-relation, the first of the 24 modes of conditionality by which all conditioning and conditioned phenomena are related in various ways. Those twenty-four modes belong to the framework of the seventh and last work of the Abhidhamma Piṭaka, the *Paṭṭhāna*,[1] and in its introductory part they are listed and explained.[2] They are also necessary for understanding how the twelve links of dependent origination (*paṭiccasamuppāda*) are related.

We reproduce here excerpts of the explanation of the root-cause condition from a treatise by an eminent Burmese scholar-monk, Ledi Sayādaw:

What is the root-cause condition (*hetu-paccaya*)? Greed, hatred, delusion, and their respective opposites, non-greed (disinterestedness), non-hatred (amity), non-delusion) (intelligence, wisdom)—these are the root-cause conditions.

What are the things that are conditioned by them? Those classes of mind and mental qualities[3] that co-exist along with greed, etc., or non greed, etc., as well as the groups of material qualities which co-exist with the

---

1. See *Conditional Relations* (*Paṭṭhāna*), tr. by U Nārada. (London: Pali Text Society, 1969).
2. Reproduced in *The Path of Purification* (*Visuddhimagga*), Ch. XVII, § 66 and in *Guide through the Abhidhamma Piṭaka*, by Ñāṇatiloka Mahāthera. Kandy: Buddhist Publication Society).
3. *Citta* and *cetasika*, consciousness and mental concomitants.

same—these are the things that are conditioned by way of root-cause condition (*hetu-paccayuppannā dhammā*). They are so called because they arise or come into existence by virtue of the root-cause condition.

Here by the phrase "the groups of material qualities which co-exist with the same" are meant the material qualities produced by kamma (*kammaja rūpa*) at the initial moment of the *hetu*-conditioned conception of a new being, as well as such material qualities as may be produced by the *hetu*-conditioned mind during the life-time. Here, by the "moment of conception" is meant the nascent instant (*uppādakkhaṇa*) of the rebirth-conception, and by "the life-time" is meant the period starting from the static instant (*ṭhitikkhaṇa*) of the rebirth. conception right on to the moment of the dying-thought.

In what sense is *hetu* to be understood? And in what sense, *paccaya*? *Hetu* is to be understood in the sense of root (*mūlaṭṭha*); and *paccaya* in the sense of assisting (*upakāraṭṭha*) in the arising, or the coming to be, of the conditionally arisen things (*paccayuppannā dhammā*).

The state of being a root (*mūlaṭṭha*) may be illustrated as follows.

Suppose a man is in love with a woman. Now, so long as he has not dispelled the lustful thought, all his acts, words and thoughts regarding this woman will be cooperating with lust (or greed), which at the same time has also under its control the material qualities produced by the same thought (e.g. *kāya-vacī-viññatti*, the "bodily or verbal intimation" of his love). We see then that all these states of mental and material qualities have their root in lustful greed for that woman. Hence, by being a *hetu* (for it acts as a root) and by being a *paccaya* (for it assists in the arising of those states of mind and body), greed is a *hetu-paccaya*, a condition aiding by way of being a root-cause. The rest may be explained and understood in the same manner—i.e., the arising of greed by way of desire for desirable (inanimate) things; the arising of hatred by way of antipathy against hateful persons or things; and the arising of delusion by way of lack of knowledge (about persons, things, and ideas not correctly perceived and understood.)

Taking a tree as illustration—we see that the roots of a tree, having firmly established themselves in the ground and drawing up sap both from soil and water, carry that sap right up to the crown of the tree, and so the tree develops and grows for a long time. In the same way, greed having firmly established itself in desirable things and drawing up the essence of pleasure and enjoyment from them, conveys that essence to the concomitant mental elements, till they burst into immoral acts and words. The same is to be said of hatred, which by way of aversion draws up the essence of displeasure and discomfort; and also of delusion, which by way of lack of knowledge cherishes the growth of the essence of vain (and deceptive) thought at many an object.

Transporting the essence thus, the three elements, greed, hatred and delusion, operate upon the component parts, so that they become happy (so to speak) and joyful at the desirable objects, etc. The component parts also become so as they are operated upon, while the co-existent material qualities share the same effect.

Coming now to the bright side—suppose the man sees danger in sensual pleasure, and gives up that lustful thought for the woman. In doing so, disinterestedness (non-greed, *alobha*) as regards her arises in him. Before this, there took place impure acts, words and thoughts, having as their root delusion (and greed); but for the time being, these are no longer present, and in their stead there arise pure acts words and thoughts, having their root in disinterestedness (non-greed). Moreover, renunciation, self-control, jhāna-exercise, or higher meditative thought, also come into being. Non-greed (*alobha*), therefore, is known as *hetupaccaya*, it being a *hetu* because it acts as a root; while it is a *paccaya* because it assists in the arising of the concomitants. The same explanation applies to the remainder of non-greed, non-hate and non-delusion, which three are opposites of greed, etc.

Here, just as the root of the tree stimulates the whole stem and its parts, so it is with non-greed (disinterestedness). It dispels the desire for desirable things, and having promoted the growth of the essence of pleasure void of greed (*lobha-viveka-sukha-rasa*), it nurtures the concomitant elements with that essence till they become so happy (so to speak) and joyful that they even reach the height of *jhānic-*, path-, or fruition-happiness. Similarly, non-hatred (amity) and non-delusion (intelligence), respectively, dispel hatred and ignorance with regard to hateful and confused (or deceptive) things, and promote the growth of the essence of pleasure void of hate and delusion. Thus the operation of the three elements, non-greed, non hatred and non-delusion, lasts for a long time, making their mental concomitants happy and joyful. The concomitant elements also become so as they are operated upon; while the coexistent groups of material qualities are affected in the same way. (pp. 1–5)

... Let say that greed springs into being within a man who desires to get money and grain. Under the influence of greed, he goes to a forest where he clears a piece of land and establishes fields, yards and gardens, and starts to work vary hard. Eventually he obtains plenty of money and grain by reason of his strenuous labours. So he takes his gains, looks after his family and performs many virtuous deeds, from which he also will be entitled to reap rewards in his future existences. In this illustration, all the mental and material states coexisting with greed are called direct effects. Apart from these, all the outcomes, results and rewards, which are to be enjoyed later on in his future existences, are called indirect effects. Of these two kinds of effects, only the former is dealt with in the Paṭṭhāna. However, the latter kind finds its place in the Suttanta discourses. "If this exists, then that happens; or because of the occurrences of this, that also takes place"—such an exposition is called "expounding by way of Suttanta."

In fact, the three states, greed, hatred and delusion, are called root conditions because they are roots whence springs the defilement of the whole animate world, of the whole inanimate world, and of the world of space. The three opposite states, non-greed, non-hatred and non-delusion, are also called root-conditions since they are the roots from which springs purification.

(pp. 117–118)

From: *Paṭṭhānuddesa Dīpanī: The Buddhist Philosophy of Relations,*

by the Venerable Ledi Sayādaw, tr. by the Venerable U Nyāna (Rangoon, 1935).[1]

---

1. *Wheel* 331/333. Some of the English terms in that treatise have been replaced by those used in this book.

Of Related Interest:

AṄGUTTARA NIKĀYA ANTHOLOGY
An anthology of discourses from the Aṅguttara Nikāya
Selected & Translated from the Pali by
Nyanaponika Thera & Bhikkhu Bodhi

This book contains an anthology of 154 selected discourses from the Pali canon. The original translation was by Nyanaponika Thera and was published in the BPS Wheel Series in three volumes. This translation has been revised by Bhikkhu Bodhi and contains his notes to the discourses.

The collection contains some of the most important and inspiring discouses of the Buddha such as the Kālāma Sutta, and many discourses with practical advice for lay people.

BP 222   260 pp.

THE VISION OF DHAMMA
Nyanaponika Thera

This volume brings between two covers the author's original writings from the BPS's Wheel and Bodhi Leaves series. These writings offer one of the most mature, comprehensive, and authoritative expressions of Buddhism by a contemporary Western monk, the co-founder of the BPS.

BP 414S   374 pp.

THE HEART OF BUDDHIST MEDITATION
Nyanaponika Thera

A modern Buddhist classic, translated into seven languages. With the combined powers of deep personal insight and clear exposition, the author conveys the essential principles making up the Buddha's way of mindfulness.

BP 509S   224 pp.

THE PATH OF PURIFICATION: VISUDDHIMAGGA
Translated by Bhikkhu Nanamoli

The *Visuddhimagga* is the most important non-canonical work of Theravada Buddhism. Written in the 5th century by Ācāriya Buddhaghosa, the book serves as a systematic encyclopaedia of Buddhist doctrine and a detailed guide to meditation. The translation by Ven. Ñāṇamoli itself ranks as an outstanding scholarly achievement.

BP 207H   950 pp.

All prices as in latest catalogue: http://www.bps.lk

THE BUDDHIST PUBLICATION SOCIETY

The BPS is an approved charity dedicated to making known the Teaching of the Buddha, which has a vital message for all people. Founded in 1958, the BPS has published a wide variety of books and booklets covering a great range of topics. Its publications include accurate annotated translations of the Buddha's discourses, standard reference works, as well as original contemporary expositions of Buddhist thought and practice. These works present Buddhism as it truly is—a dynamic force which has influenced receptive minds for the past 2500 years and is still as relevant today as it was when it first arose. For more information about the BPS and our publications, please visit our website, or contact:

Administrative Secretary
Buddhist Publication Society
P.O. Box 61
54 Sangharaja Mawatha
Kandy • Sri Lanka

E-mail: bps@bps.lk
web site: http://www.bps.lk
Tel: 0094 81 223 7283 • Fax: 0094 81 222 3679